ORTHO
START-TO-FINISH
SHEDS & GAZEBOS

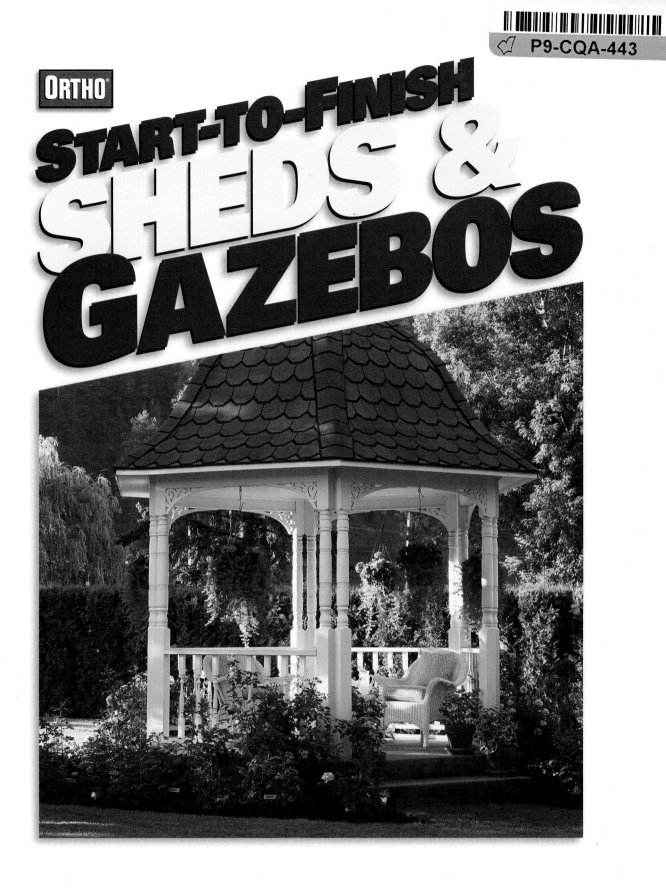

Meredith® Books
Des Moines, Iowa

Ortho® Books
An imprint of Meredith® Books

Start-to-Finish Sheds & Gazebos
Editor: Larry Johnston
Writer: Martin Miller
Senior Associate Design Director: Tom Wegner
Assistant Editor: Harijs Priekulis
Copy Chief: Terri Fredrickson
Copy and Production Editor: Victoria Forlini
Editorial Operations Manager: Karen Schirm
Managers, Book Production: Pam Kvitne,
　Marjorie J. Schenkelberg
Contributing Copy Editor: Kim Catanzarite
Technical Proofreader: Griffin M. Wall
Contributing Proofreaders: Heidi Johnson, Jim Stepp,
　Ellie Sweeney
Indexer: Barbara L. Klein
Electronic Production Coordinator: Paula Forest
Editorial and Design Assistants: Renee E. McAtee,
　Karen McFadden

Additional Editorial Contributions from
　Art Rep Services
Director: Chip Nadeau
Designer: lk Design
Illustrator: Dave Brandon
Structural Designer: Dave Morse

Meredith® Books
Editor in Chief: Linda Raglan Cunningham
Design Director: Matt Strelecki
Executive Editor, Gardening and Home Improvement:
　Benjamin W. Allen
Executive Editor, Home Improvement: Larry Erickson

Publisher: James D. Blume
Executive Director, Marketing: Jeffrey Myers
Executive Director, New Business Development:
　Todd M. Davis
Executive Director, Sales: Ken Zagor
Director, Operations: George A. Susral
Director, Production: Douglas M. Johnston
Business Director: Jim Leonard

Vice President and General Manager: Douglas J. Guendel

Meredith Publishing Group
President, Publishing Group: Stephen M. Lacy
Vice President-Publishing Director: Bob Mate

Meredith Corporation
Chairman and Chief Executive Officer: William T. Kerr

Chairman of the Executive Committee: E. T. Meredith III

Thanks
Milt Charno and Associates, specialists in decks, gazebos,
and outdoor structures.
Janet Anderson

Photographers
　(Photographers credited may retain copyright ©
　to the listed photographs.)
L = Left, R = Right, C = Center, B = Bottom, T = Top

Laurie Black: 4T, 107
Stephen Cridland: 6BR
Jay Graham: 9
Roy Inman: 5BR
Frances Litman: 13
Janet Mesic-Mackie: 6CL
John Miller/Hedrich-Blessing: 7TR
Tommy Miyasaki/deGennaro Associates: 4B
Mike Moreland: 6BL
Tim Murphy/Foto Imagery: 8, 12
M.C. Pindar: 7CL, 107B
Jessie Walker: 7CR

Cover photo: Tommy Miyasaki/deGennaro Associates

All of us at Ortho® Books are dedicated to providing you
with the information and ideas you need to enhance your
home and garden. We welcome your comments and
suggestions about this book. Write to us at:
　Meredith Corporation
　Ortho Books
　1716 Locust St.
　Des Moines, IA 50309–3023

If you would like to purchase any of our home improvement,
gardening, cooking, crafts, or home decorating and design
books, check wherever quality books are sold. Or visit us at:
meredithbooks.com

If you would like more information on other Ortho
products, call 800-225-2883 or visit us at: www.ortho.com

A simple well-proportioned shed makes an attractive addition to the landscape. Consider the interior space you need and size the building appropriately. Then locate the structure in a place that's both convenient and fitting to the scale of your yard.

Consider the overall look and character of the neighborhood when planning any outdoor structure, especially if the building will be visible across property lines. Remember that your neighbors have to live with whatever you choose too.

DESIGN AND PLANNING

Once you decide to build a shed or gazebo, you open the door to an exciting adventure in design. Decisions about appearance, size, and location are often so intertwined that you don't know where to start. You want a structure that enhances your enjoyment of the landscape or serves a useful purpose, of course. But you'll have to ask and answer many questions before you reach that goal: Where should it go? How large should it be? Will construction be difficult?

That's where this book comes in: It answers your questions about designing and constructing the shed or gazebo that best meets your needs. This chapter helps you ask the right questions and find the answers you need to plan your project. You will then find two chapters with plans for sheds and gazebos that complement any landscape. Each plan includes dimensions and illustrated step-by-step building instructions.

Think of each project as the starting point for your own adaptation; the book provides a wealth of design options you can use to customize each structure to fit into your landscape. Throughout the book you will find details that can be incorporated into any plan so your structure will be like no other.

The project plans are straightforward. All the structures are built following standard, uncomplicated construction methods, using readily available materials. None of the gazebos require the complicated layout computations and complex angles often associated with building a structure that has more than four sides.

Each plan includes a materials list, with some of the quantities translated into lineal feet or square feet to help you estimate costs. When you go to the lumberyard or home center to buy materials, take the plans with you. A structure might call for 300 square feet of siding, for example. Study the plans to determine how many pieces of lap siding or sheets of vertical siding you need, depending on what you plan to use. The lumber salesperson can help you determine amounts.

If you are new to building or your knowledge of construction methods and techniques is a little rusty, don't worry: The last chapter in the book covers basic building information; everything you need to know to complete your project.

Choose your site carefully. A location with level ground is best because it will not require extensive site preparation or expensive grading.

SHOPPING FOR STYLE

Outdoor design ideas often show up in the most surprising places—right in your own neighborhood, for example.

You may not have noticed your neighbors' garden sheds and other outdoor structures until now, but once you decide to build your own shed or gazebo, your own neighborhood is a good place to start collecting style ideas. After you've surveyed your immediate surroundings, take a look at utility buildings out in the countryside. Older outbuildings provide important clues about which styles and designs best fit the climate, terrain, and weather in your area.

Books and periodicals on gardening are great sources—even the articles that aren't about garden structures provide ideas. Sheds and gazebos often show up in photos of gorgeous gardens and landscapes. Copy or cut out pictures from various publications and keep them in a manila folder. When you're ready to design your project, go through the folder and throw away those ideas that no longer suit your needs. Choose design elements for your project from the pictures that still appeal to you.

CHOOSING A DESIGN

When choosing a design for your shed or gazebo, the appearance of the structure takes second place on the list of things you need to consider. The most important determination is: What do you want the building to do? The answer to that question affects the appearance of the project.

Screened openings make this gazebo a pleasant, bug-free place to view the garden. Steps lead down from an adjacent deck to the gazebo, which has been raised to overlook the garden.

FUNCTION AND FORM

If you want to build a structure for storage, make a list of what you want to store. A small 3×6-foot shed attached to the garage or house will be perfect for storing rakes, shovels, trowels, and bags of fertilizer. It might even be roomy enough for a medium-size push mower.

But if you have a riding mower, a garden tractor, a wheelbarrow or other large equipment, the need for space increases dramatically. You may intend to use a potting shed only for potting plants. But most potting sheds eventually become storage sheds too. So plan the shed to allow enough room for potting *and* storage. Similarly a gazebo with an 8- or 9-foot floor diameter will comfortably accommodate a family of four but quickly confines a group of party guests.

Other factors affect the design of the structure as well. For instance a small shed can have a single or double entry door but probably won't have enough wall space for a window. A larger structure allows a window and larger doors, letting in light and improving access. Windows and other elements that open up increased opportunities for design are easier to incorporate into larger buildings.

And what goes inside a shed—worktables, shelving, cabinets, and so forth—affects not only the size of the structure but also its exterior appearance.

The materials used, too, can limit design. Physical limitations complicate window installation in openings larger than about 3½ feet, for example. If you're planning an enclosed 12-foot gazebo, its 60-inch openings will require windows with a center support (unless you're willing to spend a lot of money), and you may not like the way the support breaks the line of the opening. To avoid problems plan the project in as much detail as possible before you start construction.

Built with both new and salvaged materials, this shed fits the overall look of the garden and adds its own touch of charm.

This playhouse is simply an 8×8-foot shed built on an 8×12-foot platform to provide a porch. The porch roof, trim, and colorful paint scheme disguise its utilitarian structure. When the children outgrow the playhouse, it can serve as a storage shed and potting area.

STYLE

All objects and structures possess line, form, color, and texture. How these attributes interact affects the appearance, or style, of your project. Shed styles are generally either formal or informal. Formal styles are usually characterized by straight lines, right angles, and symmetry. Informal designs have curved lines and asymmetrical elements. Coarse or natural textures are considered informal.

Attributes are often mixed in designs. Board-and-batten siding has the straight lines of a formal style, but the boards are often rough-textured, giving the siding a less-formal look. While intricate Victorian gingerbread trim is often composed of curved lines, has a smooth surface, and is painted, the overall effect is usually formal. When designing your project, consider whether your landscape leans toward the formal or informal, then build a structure in sync with that character.

A single outdoor structure can serve several purposes. The back of this 15-foot-diameter gazebo, for example, is a storage shed for toys and equipment used in a nearby pool.

INSTANT OUTDOOR STRUCTURES

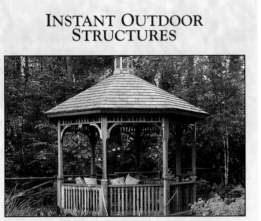

If you're short on time or motivation, consider building a kit shed or gazebo.

Ready-to-assemble gazebos come in a variety of styles. Shed kits range from basic utility sheds sold by lumberyards and home centers to designer models. Depending on the size, it's possible for two people to build a kit shed or gazebo in a weekend or two.

Buying a kit saves you time, but it's not likely to save you money. Check out the quality of materials—inspect an in-store model or one that has been built by a customer. Look for rust-resistant hardware, straight framing, defect-free lumber, and precise milling.

Redwood and cedar cost more, but their appearance and resistance to decay sometimes makes up for the expense. Make sure wood that isn't naturally decay-resistant has been treated and that posts and floor framing members are rated for ground contact.

GETTING DESIGN HELP

Design professionals often see solutions to problems at a glance. Enlisting their help can save you money in the long run. If a conference with a landscape pro results in a solution that avoids grading a slope, for example, the consultation has paid for itself. Here's a brief summary of the levels of design help you'll find in the profession.

■ Landscape architects have the most formal training and are licensed. They handle all aspects of planning and construction supervision.

■ Landscape designers tend to have strong horticultural backgrounds but are skilled in other aspects of design as well. They can help you draw up plans.

■ Nursery and garden center staff often provide suggestions on general ideas, particularly about plants and materials.

Color is an important design element and usually the first noticed. The right paint color or stain can dramatically improve the overall look of any outdoor structure.

CHOOSING A SITE

The placement of a shed or gazebo is a crucial consideration that affects the building's usefulness, as well as the character of the surrounding area.

GETTING STARTED

Go outside and stand next to your house, roughly at the middle of the wall, and casually survey your yard for what seems to be the best location for the shed or gazebo. This first step in site selection sounds almost too simple, but you'll refine the process later.

LOCATING A SHED: If you're planning to build a shed, look for a location that's convenient and logical with regard to the garden. If you have two planting beds, you could center the shed between them. This is a way to unify the garden district in your landscape. If you plan to add a new garden area that includes your new shed, treat the new addition as one area and plan accordingly. If you don't have beds and don't plan to make any, a place close to the rear or edge of the property usually makes sense. Remember that a freestanding shed is a design element in its own right—it should be located where it maintains its own identity without appearing to be an adjunct to the house or garage.

LOCATING A GAZEBO: Trust your instincts when considering the best place for your gazebo. From the moment you started thinking about building a gazebo, you probably had a notion—perhaps only dimly perceived—of where you would build it. Stand next to your house and find that spot. You may end up changing your mind, but that instinctive location is a good place to start.

REFINING THE PROCESS

No matter what kind of structure you plan to build, outline its rough dimensions on the yard with spray paint. Don't be concerned with marking the exact footprint yet— you still have some other decisions to make.

SIZING THINGS UP: First evaluate the size of the painted perimeter. Will all your current or planned equipment fit comfortably, or should you enlarge it so you don't have to crawl over things to get to the tool you want? Bring out your tools, the lawn mower, and other equipment and put it all between the painted lines to make sure it fits. For a gazebo, set your patio furniture inside the sprayed outline. Imagine the floor space as it will be when finally furnished. Does everything seem to fit? Imagine it with family and guests. Can people move around or will they be reduced to elbow room only? Change the size of the painted imprint to meet your current and planned needs.

A gazebo can stand alone in the landscape or, as in this case, become part of a porch or deck attached to the house.

THE ROOM WITH A VIEW: How the structure looks from the house and the yard undoubtedly is important, but the reverse is also true.

Stand at the planned site and observe the other elements in your yard. Even if you're building a basic shed, you probably don't want to see the utility boxes behind the garage every time you use it. And if you build a potting shed, you'll want to see an attractive view from the work space. That goes double for the views from a gazebo. Take your time and look out from every side. Changing a gazebo's location by a matter of feet often makes a significant difference in the view.

EVALUATE THE SITE AND CLIMATE

In most cases it's best to put your structure on level ground. Building on sloped ground increases the difficulty of construction, plus grading a slope is expensive. Avoid areas that require removal of large trees or rocks, preparations that often cost more than the project itself.

Consider traffic patterns in the yard and how you will use the structure. If you'll be dining outdoors frequently, locate the gazebo with easy access to the kitchen. You may need to compromise between the location that looks best and the one that works best. If privacy matters to you, take advantage of trees, fences, or an out-of-the-way site. Clear interfering tree branches before you begin

A great view is part of the pleasure provided by this gazebo. At 13½ feet in diameter, the gazebo is large enough for several guests to take in the sights at the same time. Evaluate your gazebo site carefully, then locate the structure for the best view.

construction. Stopping construction to remove a branch delays the project. And removing the branch may change the view for the worse—if it shielded the view from a neighboring house, for instance.

Take sunlight and wind into account. Watch how the sun affects the site at different times of the day and year. For a gazebo location, you may want sunlight in the morning and evening but shade during the hottest part of the day. Consider, too, the prevailing winds on your proposed site. A cool afternoon breeze may be welcome on a hot summer day, but strong gusty winds howling through an unsheltered area renders an outdoor room unusable.

When you think you've found the perfect spot, wait a week or so before beginning construction. Evaluate the site for several days and make changes until everything feels right.

BUILDING CODES AND PERMITS

Most communities have building codes to ensure safety, uniformity, and quality of construction. These codes, as well as zoning ordinances and deed restrictions, usually apply to sheds, gazebos, and other landscape structures too.

Codes may specify the setback—how close you can locate the structure to your property line. Codes may also dictate that you use certain materials and lumber of specified dimensions in the construction of your project. In addition, the maximum amount of space allowed between balusters on a gazebo railing is usually prescribed. (This spacing is regulated to prevent children from getting their heads caught between the balusters).

When you plan your project, check with your local zoning and building departments to see what restrictions apply.

PAINT THE LOCATION

Once your plans are drawn and you're ready to take them into the landscape, buy a couple of cans of upside-down spray paint for marking.

This ground-marking paint was developed primarily for road maintenance purposes. Unlike ordinary household spray paint, which won't work if inverted, this paint works upside down and is an excellent way to mark postholes and the perimeter of your project.

MAKING PLANS

BASE MAP, NEW PATH, AND PLANTING BEDS

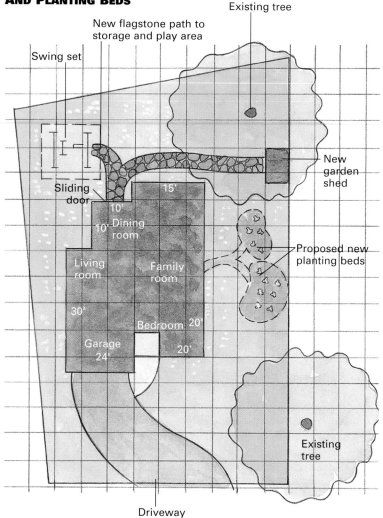

Existing tree

New flagstone path to storage and play area

Swing set

Sliding door

New garden shed

15'

10'

10'   Dining room

Living room

Family room

Proposed new planting beds

30'

Bedroom   20'

Garage 24'   20'

Existing tree

Driveway

Even the most experienced carpenters don't start a construction project without some form of plan on paper. The plan for your shed or gazebo could be anything from a simple sketch for a single building to a complete scheme for remodeling the landscape.

Even if you intend to build one of the structures shown in this book exactly, you should start with a plan that shows where you will locate it in your yard. This not only helps guide your construction, it also might be necessary to receive approval from your building department. If your project is subject to local construction codes, you may need detailed drawings that designate the size and quality of the materials.

MAKING A BASE MAP

Start with a base map—an overhead diagram of your property that includes property lines and major features, such as the house, outbuildings, and trees. The easiest way to go about developing a base map is to make a scaled copy of your plat or other official map. You might find such a map among the papers from the closing of the purchase of your home. If you can't find it, get a copy from your county tax assessor.

WHAT THE BASE MAP SHOULD SHOW:

■ The distance of major elements, such as trees, the house, a garden shed, or a detached garage, from the property lines and from each other.
■ Location of doors and windows and what rooms they are in.

WALL FRAMING PLAN

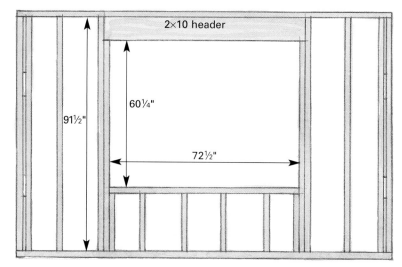

2×10 header

91½"

60¼"

72½"

LOCALIZE YOUR FOUNDATION

Most of the projects in this book are built on a foundation of 4×4 posts set below the local frost line, but you can adapt the plans to fit other foundations. Where frost is not a threat or where bedrock prohibits excavation, for instance, you can set the posts on concrete piers.

Check with your building department for requirements appropriate to the local geology and climate.

■ The overhang of roof eaves beyond the walls of the house (if you are building a new deck or patio as part of the project).
■ Downspouts and runoff direction.
■ The direction and pitch of slopes or major changes in ground level.

ANALYZING YOUR SITE

Making a site analysis on your base map is a good idea even if you're only adding a single structure to your landscape. A site analysis helps ensure, for example, that you're not putting your structure in a low, boggy spot which could make construction and access difficult.

To make the site analysis, take the base map outside and mark it with the assets (things you want to keep) and liabilities (things you want to change). A thorough site analysis includes:
■ Views you want to maintain or hide.
■ Nearby sources of noise, day and night.
■ Elements to increase privacy.
■ Drainage that needs correction.
■ Grading that needs to be done to improve the use of your property.
■ Direction of prevailing winds.
■ Sun and shade patterns.
■ Natural traffic patterns.
■ Location of underground utilities. (Call your utilities to locate and mark them.)

The results of your site analysis help you decide whether to build your shed or gazebo on a frame floor, as shown in the plans, or on a concrete slab. If the ground slopes at the project site, a frame floor will be easier to build and will not require expensive grading.

BUBBLE AND MASTER PLANS

A bubble plan shows how you use different areas in your yard. A master plan shows all the elements in the landscape design, both the hard scape and the planting beds. Both plans are handy if you are building a structure as part of a landscape makeover. If you are simply adding a shed or gazebo to an existing plan, skip these plans and make scale drawings of the project itself.

To make the bubble plan, tape tracing paper over your base map. Mark different areas of the yard by drawing circles or ovals, then label how each one is used. Tape another piece of tracing paper over the base map to make the master plan. Draw all the landscape details on the plan.

FINISHED WALL PLAN

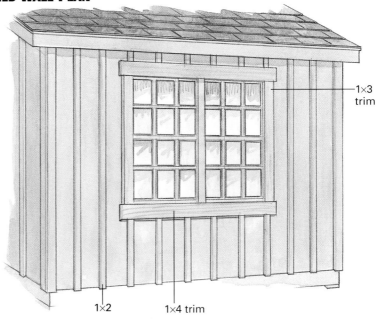

1×3 trim

1×2   1×4 trim

CONSTRUCTION PLANS

Once you have decided on the use, size, and location of your project, prepare drawings of the structure. Drawings for each of the projects in this book are sufficiently detailed, so you can begin building without further sketching. The projects also include information on the modifications you can make. If you decide to make modifications, sketch them before ordering materials.

Draw framing elevations, as shown on the opposite page, and finished elevations, as shown above. Such drawings help you think out the building design and force you to concentrate on the actual construction process rather than design decisions.

HIGH-TECH PLANNING

If you're planning to redesign your landscape, consider using landscape-design software to simplify the job. The programs are easy to use, flexible, and can speed your progress from base plan to final design. You'll find them especially useful when making changes—you can alter your plans without having to redraw them.

The programs calculate dimensions of each structure, create side elevations and three-dimensional views, make materials lists, and create repeating patterns on walkways. You can even place trees and shrubs where you want them.

Home improvement and gardening magazines often review the newest programs. You can buy software from computer stores. Or check out local home improvement or building supply centers—many offer computer design services without cost if you purchase your materials from them.

The plants surrounding a garden shed connect it to the landscape design. Enlist all the design elements—color, texture, line, and form—when developing a planting plan.

PLANTING THE SITE

Without a connection to the other elements in your yard, even the most attractive shed or gazebo ends up looking like an add-on in your landscape. With the addition of plants, however, you can easily integrate your new outdoor structure into the landscape.

Foliage offers a pleasing contrast in both color and texture to the materials used to build your shed or gazebo and also provides a gentle visual transition to the rest of the yard.

SELECTING PLANTS

Plant selection depends on your personal preference. You might like contrast—a bed of white blooms in front of a dark-stained redwood shed—or complements—a white flower bed around the base of a white Victorian gazebo that extends to the green lawn. Red tulips or roses set off a white structure, making it a stronger visual accent, while shrubs along the side of a shed help break up the lines of horizontal siding and add a textural contrast. Consider combining textural and color variations—for instance, large yellow variegated foliage to smartly set off a hunter green shed.

PLANTS THAT LIKE THE SUN

Common/Botanical Name	Height	Color	Zone	Comments
Alpine lady's mantle (*Alchemilla alpina*)	6"	Chartreuse	3–4	Quick to spread
Rockcress (*Arabis caucasica*)	8"	White	4–8	Mat-forming
Marsh marigold (*Caltha palustris*)	15"	Yellow	5–7	Likes wet soils
Carpathian bellflower (*Campanula carpatica*)	9–12"	Violet/White	3–8	Fast-growing, clump-forming
Plumbago (*Ceratostigma plumbaginoides*)	8"	Blue	5–8	Good ground cover
Cheddar pink (*Dianthus gratianopolitanus*)	6"	Pink	3–9	Mat-forming, heat-tolerant, fragrant
Aspen daisy (*Erigeron speciosus* var. *macranthus*)	8"	Lavender	2–8	Good for crevices, steps
Dwarf blue fescue (*Festuca glauca*)	8"	Silvery foliage	4–8	Grows in tufts for textural contrast
Cranesbill (*Geranium sanguineum striatum*)	8"	Light pink	4–6	A virtually carefree ground cover
Rose mallow (*Hibiscus moscheutos*)	5'	White/Pink/Red	5–9	Likes wet soils
Japanese iris (*Iris ensata*)	5'	Blues/Pinks/Whites	4–9	Thrives in moist, acid soil
Sword-leaf inula (*Inula ensifolia* 'Compacta')	10"	Yellow	4–8	Long-lasting flowers
Moss phlox (*Phlox subulata*)	6"	Pink/Lavender/White	3–9	Moss-like foliage, evergreen mats
Himalayan fleece flower (*Polygonum affine*)	6–9"	Creamy white	4–9	Tolerates some foot traffic
Soapwort (*Saponaria officinalis*)	2–3"	Rose-pink	4–7	Mat-forming, virtually pest-free
Sedum (*Sedum spectabile* 'Vera Jameson')	10–12"	Dusky pink	3–10	Long-season interest
Wild thyme (*Thymus serpyllum*)	1–8"	White/Pink/Violet	3–8	Four-season interest, virtually pest-free
Creeping verbena (*Verbena* hybrids)	12"	Purple	6–10	All-season blooms

GET TO KNOW THE CULTURE

Culture, the conditions of soil, light, and water in which a plant thrives, is the most important consideration in selecting plants. Plants suited to the conditions in your landscape are more likely to grow successfully. And though plants native to your area have a greater chance of success than those from different regions, they are not the only good choices. The staff at your local garden center will help you choose plants that will work in your setting.

The tables on these pages list just a few plants suitable for sunny and shaded areas. The Zone designation represents the areas of the country in which the plant grows best, based on climatic conditions in the region. Turn to the U.S. Department of Agriculture climatic zones map on page 109 to find the zone in which you live and compare it with the designations on the chart. There's a little leeway in the designations. If you live in Zone 4, for example, you may still be able to grow plants from warmer zones. Check with your garden center to be sure.

Plants and climbing roses naturally tie this gazebo to the landscape. Instead of standing out, it becomes an integral part of the garden.

PLANTS THAT PREFER SHADE

Common/Botanical Name	Height	Color	Zone	Comments
Lady's mantle (*Alchemilla mollis*)	12"	Chartreuse	4–8	Moderate growth rate
Dwarf goatsbeard (*Aruncus aethusifolius*)	8–12"	White	4–8	Flowers spike above foliage mounds
Astilbe hybrid ('Inshirach Pink')	10"	Pink	4–8	Deep green foliage
Male wood fern (*Dryopteris filix-mas*)	3–4'	Dark green	4–8	Good for shady woodlands
Barrenwort (*Epimedium × rubrum*)	10"	Red	5–8	Slow spreader, long-season interest
Hosta/Hosta nakaiana ('Golden Tiara')	8–12"	Purple	3–9	Small, gold, heart-shaped leaves
Dwarf crested iris (*Iris cristata*)	6"	Pale blue	3–8	Excellent for dry shade
Forget-me-not (*Myosotis scorpioides*)	6–8"	Light blue	3–8	Very fast growth
New Zealand flax (*Phormium tenax*)	7'	Rusty bronze	8–10	Unexcelled for color
Solomon's seal (*Polygonatum*)	24"	Yellow foliage	4–9	Tolerates dry conditions
Bethlehem sage (*Pulmonaria saccharata*)	12"	Blue	3–7	Speckled foliage
Meadow rue (*Thalictrum kiusianum*)	4–6"	Lavender	4–9	Gray-green foliage
Allegheny foam flower (*Tiarella cordifolia*)	6"	White/Pale pink	3–8	Tolerates light foot traffic
Sweet violet (*Viola odorata*)	8"	Violet/Rose/White	6–8	Unsurpassed for fragrance

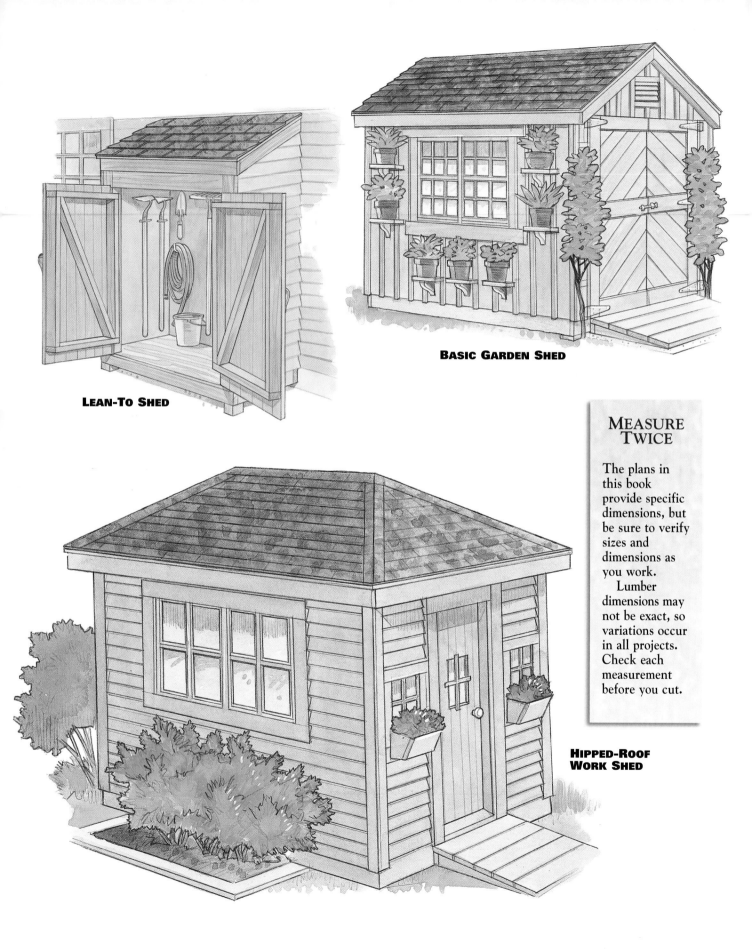

LEAN-TO SHED

BASIC GARDEN SHED

HIPPED-ROOF WORK SHED

MEASURE TWICE

The plans in this book provide specific dimensions, but be sure to verify sizes and dimensions as you work.

Lumber dimensions may not be exact, so variations occur in all projects. Check each measurement before you cut.

DESIGNING AND BUILDING SHEDS

Over time, most people accumulate more tools, equipment, and supplies for outdoor maintenance than they can comfortably store on the patio or in a corner of the garage. That's when it's time to consider a shed.

More than just an outdoor closet, a shed can house a workshop or a play area, or it can be a comfortable place to putter and take a break from daily concerns. A shed changes the appearance of your yard and may lead to a new landscape design.

When you build a shed, think big from the start. In just a few years you'll probably outgrow a shed that seemed too big when you built it, so plan for the future.

All the shed designs in this chapter follow the same basic construction sequence and easily can be built to any size and with any design accents you like. Whether you're looking for a basic shed, a small storage unit attached to the house, a hipped-roof work space, or a place just for potting and puttering around, you'll find a shed design here that meets your needs.

POTTING SHED

LEAN-TO SHED

If rakes, shovels, and other outdoor tools usually end up leaning against your house or shoved into a corner of the garage, this medium-size lean-to shed is an easy way to corral them. You can build it in a weekend at little cost.

This simple shed hangs on a garage or house wall, so you could finish the exterior to match the house or garage siding. (If you prefer, build it as a freestanding shed by building a stud wall for the back with a top plate to support the joists. Install sheathing and siding on the back wall to complete the shed.)

MATERIALS LIST

FOUNDATION, FLOOR, AND WALLS
■ Posts(check local codes)	4×4×8', 2
■ Joists	2×6×8', 5
■ Floor (¾" plywood)	4×8, 1
■ Studs, plates, rafters, header	2×4×8', 23
	2×4×6', 6
■ Siding	300 sq. ft.
■ Trim	1×8×8', 7

ROOF
■ Area	30 sq. ft.
■ Shingles	½ square
■ Roof (½" plywood)	4×8, 1

LEAN-TO SHED (PERSPECTIVE VIEW)

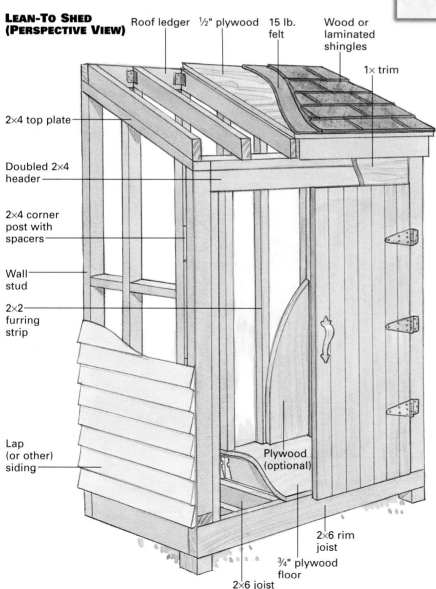

- Roof ledger
- ½" plywood
- 15 lb. felt
- Wood or laminated shingles
- 1× trim
- 2×4 top plate
- Doubled 2×4 header
- 2×4 corner post with spacers
- Wall stud
- 2×2 furring strip
- Lap (or other) siding
- Plywood (optional)
- 2×6 rim joist
- ¾" plywood floor
- 2×6 joist

If you like, add a worktable supported by diagonal 2×4s to make a potting shed. If you modify the design or dimensions of the structure, be sure to make a scale drawing of the unit before beginning its construction. Use naturally resistant woods or pressure-treated lumber rated for ground contact for the posts and floor framing. Use exterior-grade plywood for the floor. For more information on basic building techniques, refer to pages 62–107

MARKING THE LOCATION

The shed attaches to an existing wall with two ledgers—a 2×4 for the roof and a 2×6 for the floor. Locate the shed so the roof ledger is centered on the studs of the house wall. Look for a nail line in the siding or use a stud finder to locate them. You can install either ledger first, but it is often easier to mark the location of the roof ledger and drop a plumb bob to mark the position of the floor ledger. If your house or garage has lap siding, plan the height of the roof ledger so the shed's siding lines up with that on the house.

LAYING OUT THE SHED LOCATION

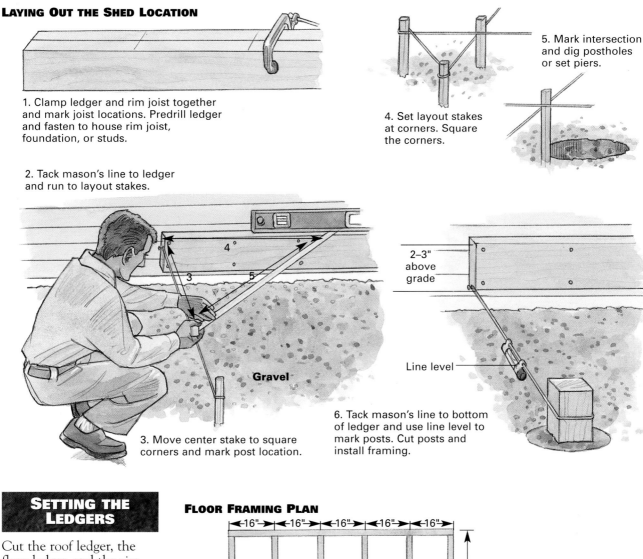

1. Clamp ledger and rim joist together and mark joist locations. Predrill ledger and fasten to house rim joist, foundation, or studs.

2. Tack mason's line to ledger and run to layout stakes.

3. Move center stake to square corners and mark post location.

Gravel

4. Set layout stakes at corners. Square the corners.

5. Mark intersection and dig postholes or set piers.

2–3" above grade

Line level

6. Tack mason's line to bottom of ledger and use line level to mark posts. Cut posts and install framing.

SETTING THE LEDGERS

Cut the roof ledger, the floor ledger, and the rim joist to length and clamp them together with their top edges flush. Starting at one end, mark the tops of the boards at 16-inch intervals. The marks on the 2×4 correspond to the rafters; those on the 2×6s indicate the locations for the centers of the joist hangers. Unclamp the boards and install the floor ledger, as illustrated at right and on page 18, with the bottom of the ledger about 3 inches above the ground. This height allows sufficient ventilation to prevent rot and mildew yet isn't so high that it requires a step into the shed. Install the roof ledger directly above the floor ledger.

FLOOR FRAMING PLAN

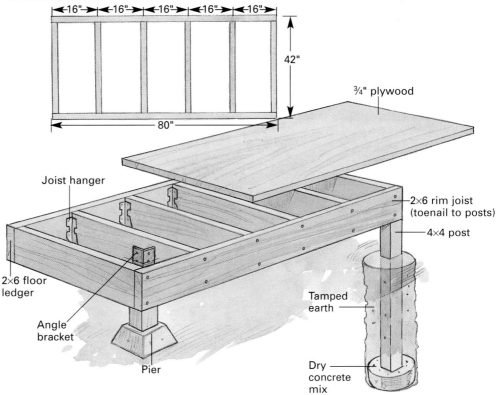

16" 16" 16" 16" 16"

42"

80"

¾" plywood

Joist hanger

2×6 floor ledger

Angle bracket

Pier

2×6 rim joist (toenail to posts)

4×4 post

Tamped earth

Dry concrete mix

LEAN-TO SHED
continued

FILLING IN THE GAPS

The floor ledger must be mounted on the same plane as the house siding, which is easy if the siding extends past the ledger location. But if the ledger attaches to the building foundation, install spacer boards behind it to bring the ledger flush, as shown in the "Ledger with Overhanging Siding" illustration below. If the position of the roof ledger puts the floor ledger partly on the siding and partly on the foundation, install spacers under the lower section of the ledger. Then countersink the fasteners for the spacer boards so the ledger lies flat.

PREPARING THE GRADE

Once the ledger is in place, excavate the area 4 inches deep, extending about 4 feet from the wall. Cover the area with landscape fabric and cover the fabric with coarse crushed stone to discourage weeds and to provide good drainage.

SETTING THE POSTS

Mark the location of the supporting posts or piers. (Local codes may specify which type of foundation to use.) Square the locations with the a 3-4-5 triangle, as shown on page 17. You may have to take down the mason's lines when you dig the postholes but put them back up for guidance when you set the posts.

Whatever foundation you employ, leave about a foot of post standing above grade. Stretch a line from the bottom of the floor ledger to each post. Level the line with a line level, and mark the posts. Cut them square at the mark with a reciprocating saw.

BUILDING THE FLOOR

Center the joist hangers on the marks you made on the ledger and rim joist. Toenail the rim joist to the posts, then face-nail the end joists, reinforcing them with angle brackets. Then place the joists in the hangers. Fasten down the plywood floor with 10d nails spaced 6 inches apart on the perimeter and every 10 inches in the field.

INSTALLING THE LEDGERS

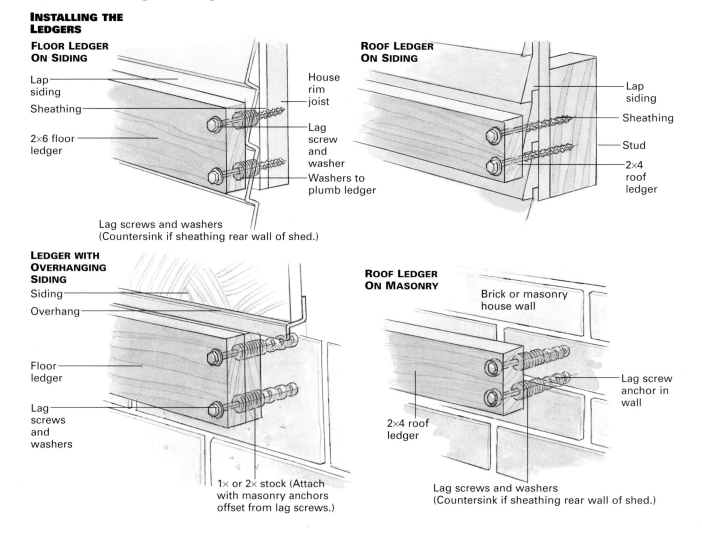

FLOOR LEDGER ON SIDING
Lap siding
Sheathing
2×6 floor ledger
House rim joist
Lag screw and washer
Washers to plumb ledger
Lag screws and washers (Countersink if sheathing rear wall of shed.)

ROOF LEDGER ON SIDING
Lap siding
Sheathing
Stud
2×4 roof ledger

LEDGER WITH OVERHANGING SIDING
Siding
Overhang
Floor ledger
Lag screws and washers
1× or 2× stock (Attach with masonry anchors offset from lag screws.)

ROOF LEDGER ON MASONRY
Brick or masonry house wall
Lag screw anchor in wall
2×4 roof ledger
Lag screws and washers (Countersink if sheathing rear wall of shed.)

CONSTRUCTING THE SIDEWALLS

Following the framing plan at right, preassemble the sidewall units. The blocking allows you to install any kind of siding on the shed, but you can leave it out for lap siding. Fasten the sidewalls to the floor and the house or garage wall. Toenail the roof ledger into the top plate to tie them together.

FURRING THE BACK WALL

You can leave the exterior house or garage wall that is exposed inside the shed as is, but installing 2×2 furring strips and sheathing allows more shelf and storage options. Place a furring strip adjacent to each sidewall to provide a nailing surface for the sheathing at both ends. If you add perforated hardboard, place 1× spacers between the hardboard and the sheathing to leave space to insert the hangers.

BUILDING THE FRONT WALL

As shown in the framing plan at right, the front wall consists of two jack studs, a header, and a top plate. The header is built from two 2×4s with ½-inch plywood spacers to make it 3½ inches thick. This particular design accommodates the double door illustrated on page 21 and other doors as well. (See additional door plans on page 103.) To provide for a narrower door, add jack studs to the opening. Preassemble the wall, place it between the sidewall corner posts, and nail it in place.

ERECTING THE SIDE WALLS

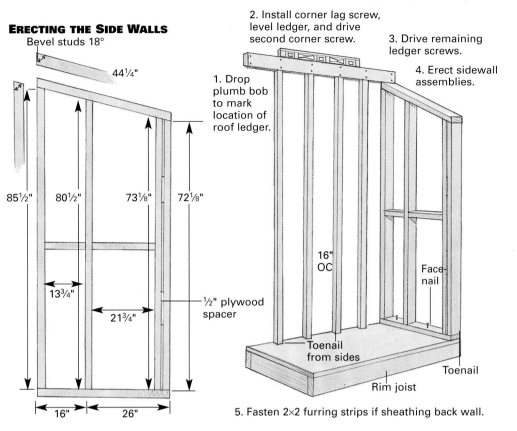

Bevel studs 18°

44¼"

85½"   80½"   73⅛"   72⅛"

13¾"

21¾"

½" plywood spacer

16"   26"

2. Install corner lag screw, level ledger, and drive second corner screw.

3. Drive remaining ledger screws.

4. Erect sidewall assemblies.

1. Drop plumb bob to mark location of roof ledger.

16" OC

Face-nail

Toenail from sides

Toenail

Rim joist

5. Fasten 2×2 furring strips if sheathing back wall.

INSTALLING THE FRONT WALL

1. Measure and cut front-wall framing.

2. Nail jack studs to corner posts.

3. Toenail header to jack studs and corner posts.

4. Face-nail top plate to header and toenail to sidewall top plate.

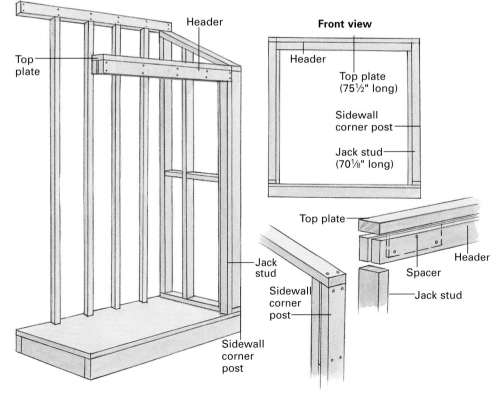

Header

Top plate

Front view

Header

Top plate (75½" long)

Sidewall corner post

Jack stud (70⅛" long)

Top plate

Header

Spacer

Jack stud

Jack stud

Sidewall corner post

Sidewall corner post

LEAN-TO SHED

continued

SIDING, ROOFING, AND TRIMMING THE SHED

Install the siding before the roof for added strength and structural stability, but fasten the end rafters in place first so you can measure and attach the siding accurately. Attach the siding with rustproof nails.

Install the rafters and cut the roof sheathing from exterior-grade plywood (46½ × 82 inches for the shed shown). The rafters do not have a bird's-mouth cut because the short span and relatively small roof size do not require the added surface support. Refer to the illustration below and the instructions on pages 90–92, then cover the sheathing with 15-pound felt paper and laminated composition shingles, shakes, or treated wood shingles. Untreated wood shingles require open sheathing to permit adequate air circulation (see pages 94–96). Install flashing where the shed roof meets the house or garage siding, and install metal drip edges at the rakes and eaves if you are installing composition shingles.

The width of the trim on the front wall varies depending on the kind of siding you use. A 1×6 might be sufficient with ½-inch siding. In most cases, however, you'll have to measure the combined thickness of the jack stud, the sidewall, and the siding, then rip the trim from a 1×8.

ROOFING, SIDING, TRIM, AND DOORS

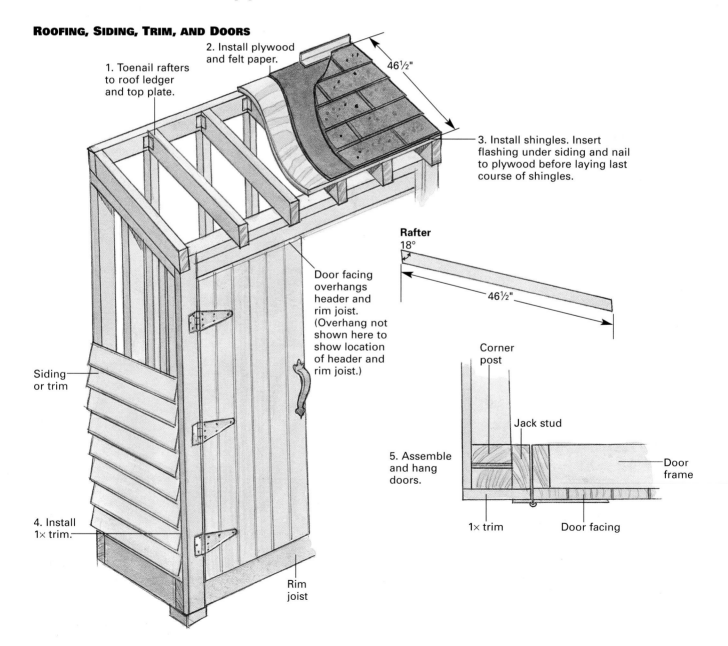

1. Toenail rafters to roof ledger and top plate.

2. Install plywood and felt paper.

46½"

3. Install shingles. Insert flashing under siding and nail to plywood before laying last course of shingles.

Door facing overhangs header and rim joist. (Overhang not shown here to show location of header and rim joist.)

Rafter
18°
46½"

Siding or trim

4. Install 1× trim.

Rim joist

5. Assemble and hang doors.

Corner post

Jack stud

Door frame

1× trim

Door facing

ASSEMBLING THE DOORS

The doors are built with 2×4 box frames faced with 1×6 planking. For easy opening and closing, each door is ¼ inch shorter than the opening and ¼ inch narrower than half the width of the opening to allow a ⅛-inch space on all sides. Door construction is shown at right.

The planking extends 3 inches above and below the door frame so it covers both the header and most of the rim joist, which would otherwise be exposed. The header and rim joist also act as stops for the doors in this design.

■ **DIAGONAL BRACING:** The door in the illustration goes in the left side of the opening. When viewed from the front, the hinges will be on the left side and the 2×4 diagonal extends up from the hinge side at the bottom. The brace for the right-side door also runs from the hinge (right side) to the upper left corner of the frame. The triangle thus formed on each door supports the center to keep the doors from sagging at the middle.

Install the door with T- or strap hinges that will allow at least two screws to be driven into the door frame. Use 3-inch screws to attach the hinges to the door and through the trim into the jack stud.

DOOR DETAIL

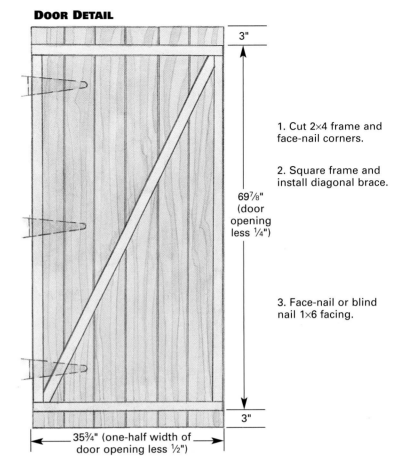

3"

69⅞" (door opening less ¼")

3"

1. Cut 2×4 frame and face-nail corners.

2. Square frame and install diagonal brace.

3. Face-nail or blind nail 1×6 facing.

35¾" (one-half width of door opening less ½")

DESIGNING YOUR OWN TRELLISES

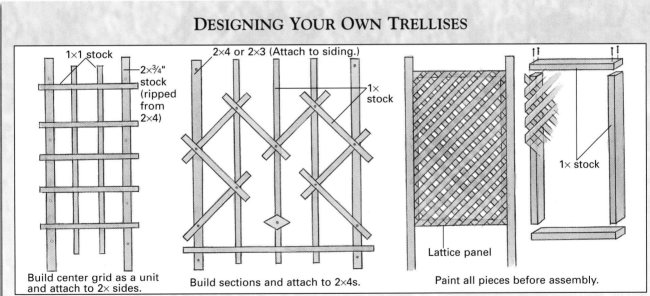

1×1 stock

2×¾" stock (ripped from 2×4)

2×4 or 2×3 (Attach to siding.)

1× stock

1× stock

Lattice panel

1× stock

Build center grid as a unit and attach to 2× sides.

Build sections and attach to 2×4s.

Paint all pieces before assembly.

Small details dramatically enhance the appearance of even a small structure, such as the lean-to shed described in this section. Lattice panels are easy-to-construct accents that don't overwhelm the structure. The designs shown above are examples of the kind of lattice patterns you can make. By combining the strips at different angles, building panels of different widths, and installing similar panels on other structures, it's easy to create a design rhythm and a unity within your landscape plan. This is especially useful for making a new structure fit in with existing structures. Lattice comes in different widths. For most applications, ⅜-inch strips hold up and resist warping better than narrower stock. For ease of installation, buy premade lattice panels that attach to a simple frame.

BASIC GARDEN SHED

Built on a 10×12-foot area, this versatile garden shed is both practical and stylish. Its board-and-batten siding complements many landscape styles. The plain expanse of siding becomes more interesting with the double doors and their diagonal facing and with the large 5×6-foot window trimmed with 1×6s and 1×4s. The stud walls accept any siding, so you can give the building any look you want.

The large 6-foot doorway and 120 square feet of floor area render this shed suitable for storing a riding mower while leaving plenty of room for other garden equipment.

This design is the basis for other sheds illustrated in this chapter. Build the structures as shown or modify them to suit your needs. If you do customize a plan, make detailed scaled drawings of your design.

MATERIALS LIST

FOUNDATION, FLOOR, AND WALLS

■ Posts (check local codes)	4×4×8', 4	
■ Joists, ramp stringers, ledger	2×8×10', 11	
	2×8×12', 6	
■ Floor (¾" plywood)	4×8, 4	
■ Studs, plates, blocking	2×4×8', 48	
	2×4×10', 10	
	2×4×12', 6	
■ Header	2×10×12', 2	
■ Siding	325 sq. ft.	
■ Trim	1×4, 54'	
	1×3, 32'	
	1×6, 15'	

ROOF

■ Area	200 sq. ft.
■ Shingles	2½ squares
■ Rafters	2×6×14', 12
■ Roof (½" plywood)	4×8, 8
■ Fascia	1×8×14', 2

GARDEN SHED (PERSPECTIVE VIEW)

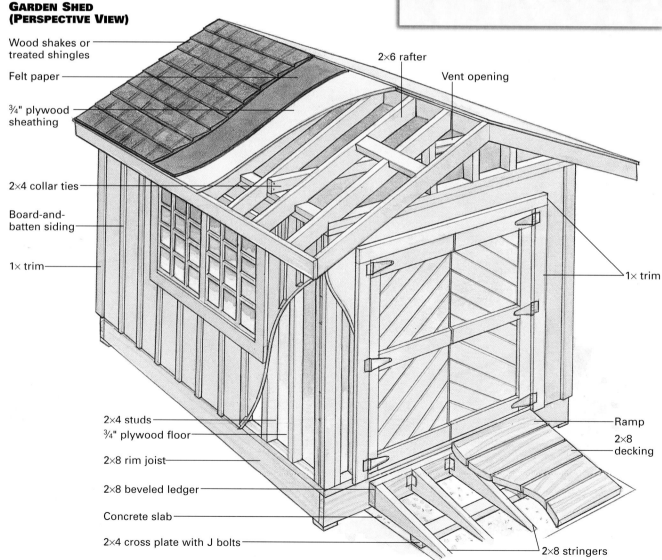

Wood shakes or treated shingles

Felt paper

¾" plywood sheathing

2×4 collar ties

Board-and-batten siding

1× trim

2×6 rafter

Vent opening

1× trim

2×4 studs

¾" plywood floor

2×8 rim joist

2×8 beveled ledger

Concrete slab

2×4 cross plate with J bolts

Ramp

2×8 decking

2×8 stringers

Whether you build exactly from the plans or modify the design, pay particular attention to the window opening. Before you assemble the window wall, determine the exact rough opening specifications of the unit you will install. A 5×6-foot window may require a rough opening larger or smaller than 60×72 inches. If you plan to install a salvaged window, get the window first, then cut the rough opening ½ to 1 inch taller and wider than the window frame.

LAYING OUT THE SITE

Lay out the site by assembling the 2×6 frame, as shown at right. Doing so produces fast, accurate results. (See "Building a Ramp" on page 24 for information on preparing the site for a ramp into the shed.)

■ **SET UP AND SQUARE:** Set up the frame and square it as shown. Then mark the perimeter and post locations with spray marking paint.

■ **PREPARE THE SITE:** Remove the frame, dig the postholes, and remove about 4 inches of soil, 6 inches in hard clay. Lay landscape fabric in the excavation, overlapping the seams 10 to 12 inches. Then fill the site to grade with coarse crushed gravel. The fabric and gravel fill prevent weeds from germinating and let the site drain quickly. Set the posts, then cut them 2 to 3 inches above grade to allow air circulation under the shed to help prevent the frame from rotting. (For more information on site preparation and foundation work, see pages 80–81.)

FRAMING THE FLOOR

■ **CUT AND MARK RIM JOISTS:** To make sure the joists run parallel to each other, clamp the rim joists together with their ends flush and mark both of them at 16-inch intervals. Center the joist hangers on the marks.

■ **BUILD THE FRAME:** Tack the perimeter joists to the posts, and recheck the frame for square by taking diagonal measurements. The frame is square if the measurements are equal. Tap the frame to square it and drive the nails home.

■ **INSTALL JOISTS AND FLOOR:** Place the joists in the hangers. Cover the floor framing with

LAYING OUT THE SITE

1. Set 2×6 layout frame and stake corners.

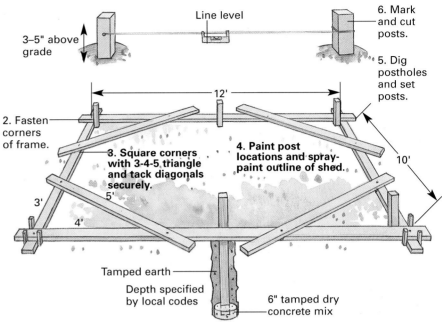

¾-inch exterior-grade plywood, starting with a full sheet set flush with a frame corner. Stagger the joints of the next course and the final half-sheet course. Leave a ⅛-inch gap between the sheets—an 8d nail makes a handy, accurate spacing tool. (See pages 82–83 for more information about floor framing.)

FRAMING THE FLOOR

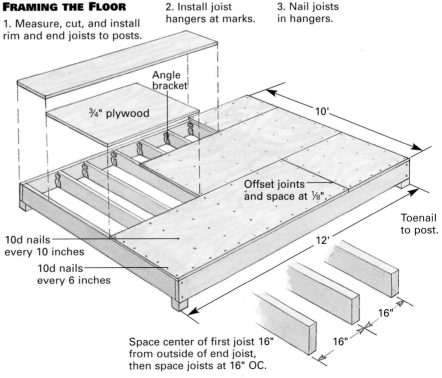

BASIC GARDEN SHED
continued

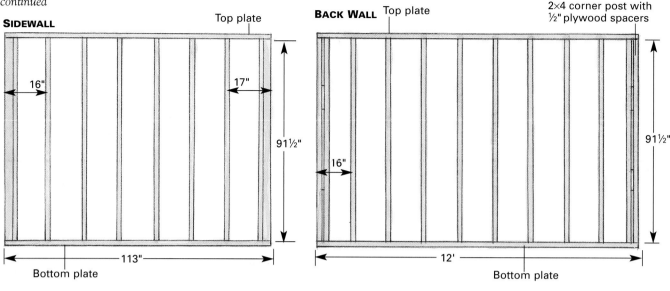

SIDEWALL

Top plate

16"

17"

91½"

113"

Bottom plate

BACK WALL   Top plate

2×4 corner post with
½" plywood spacers

16"

91½"

12'

Bottom plate

FRAMING THE WALLS

Following the framing plans on these two pages, cut the lumber for one wall at a time and assemble it. Build the walls on the floor, then raise them into place. Starting with the back wall, build each wall, raise it, and brace it temporarily to give yourself room to work. Vertical siding requires 2×4 blocking between the studs, but you can install it later. (See pages 84–85 for more about walls.)

■ **MARK THE PLATES:** Align the top and bottom plates and mark them for each stud location, including king studs, jack studs, and cripple studs. Build each corner post as a unit and treat it as a single stud.

■ **RAISE THE BACK WALL:** When you stand the wall up, fasten it to the floor and brace it with 1×3 braces nailed to the studs and the floor, making sure it's plumb. Temporarily nail a 1×3 diagonally across the wall to keep it square.

■ **SETTING THE SIDEWALLS:** Assemble and attach the sidewall and door wall next, then complete the framing with the front wall. Brace each one plumb and square. Leave the braces in place until you install roofing or siding, whichever you choose to do first.

■ **CENTERING A WINDOW:** If you are installing a window that's larger or smaller than the one specified here, you probably will have to alter the stud layout to center the window. It's best to lay out window framing on paper before marking the plates.

To center a window, subtract the width of its rough opening (the length of the header) from the total length of the wall. Draw in the jack studs, the header, and the king studs, centering them on the wall sketch. Then

measure 16-inch intervals from each end until you reach the king stud that supports the window, keeping the space between any two studs at 16 inches or less. Transfer the dimensions to the top and bottom plates.

■ **TYING THE CORNERS:** Mark the rafter centers on the cap plates and install the cap plates. Lap the cap plates over the top plates at the corners, as shown at right. Center the rafter ties on the cap plate at rafter locations.

BUILDING A RAMP

A ramp, as shown in the illustration on page 22, makes getting a lawn mower or other wheeled equipment into the shed easier. When you prepare the site, pour a 4-inch-thick grade-level slab 6 feet wide (or a little wider than the doorway), extending 4 feet from the rim joist. Then build the ramp later. (See pages 80–83 for information on concrete slabs.)

To build the ramp, saw a 10-degree bevel on the top edge of a 6-foot-long 2×8. Lag-bolt the piece, bevel facing up and out, to the rim joist in front of the door opening. Cut five 2×8 stringers 41 inches long that taper from 7¼ inches wide at one end to a point at the other. (You can probably cut two from one 42-inch piece of 2×8.) Attach the stringers to the beveled 2×8 with angle brackets. Install 2×8 planking on the ramp. Bevel the leading edge of the first plank to reduce the bump onto the ramp.

FRONT WALL

Top plate   2×10 header   Add trimmers here to make opening narrower.

58"

Jack stud

80"

75½"

78½"

Cripple stud

91½"

16"   16"

20½"

12'

Note: Rough opening will vary from one window to another. Add trimmer studs or alter stud spacing to adjust width and center the window. Change length of cripple studs to modify opening height.

DOOR WALL

Top plate   2×10 header

73½"

80¼"

Jack stud

91½"

70½"

16"   81"   16"

113"

ERECTING THE WALLS

Cap plate

Alternate overlaps to bond walls.

Top plate

Corner post

1. Assemble front wall and brace upright.

2. Assemble remaining walls, fastening sidewalls to corner posts.

Cap plate

2×10 door header

3. Tie walls together with overlapping cap plates.

2×10 header

Wall top plate

Corner post

Temporary brace

Sidewall stud

Sill

Cripples

End joist

Bottom plate

Rim joist

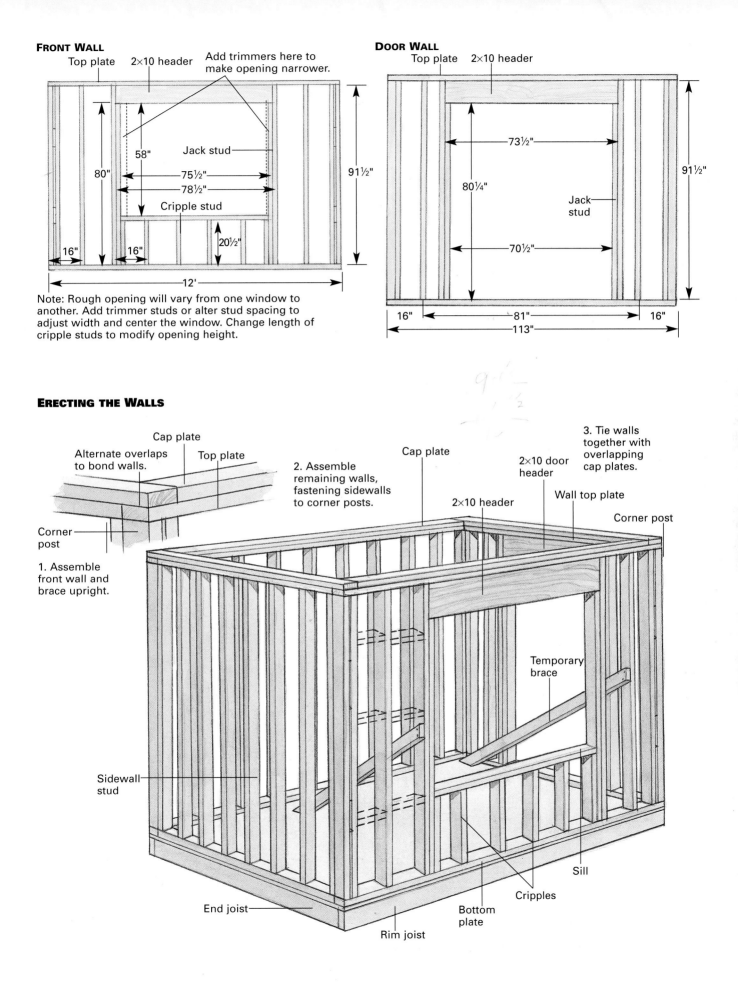

BASIC GARDEN SHED
continued

ROOF FRAMING PLAN

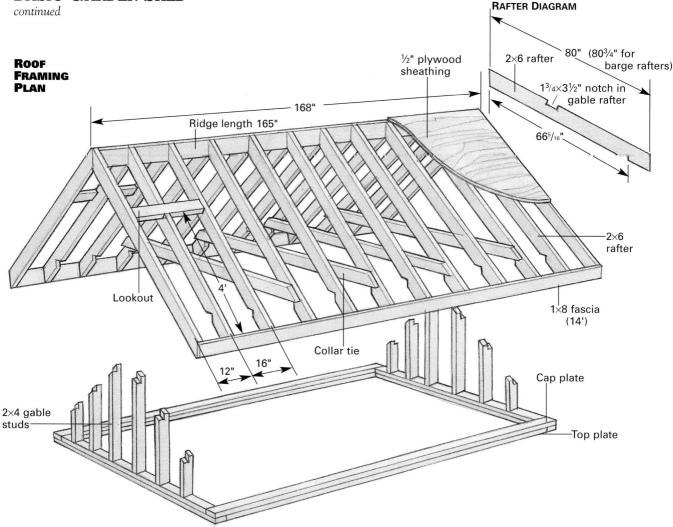

RAFTER DIAGRAM

½" plywood sheathing

2×6 rafter

80" (80¾" for barge rafters)

1¾×3½" notch in gable rafter

66⁵/₁₆"

168"

Ridge length 165"

Lookout

4'

Collar tie

12"   16"

2×4 gable studs

2×6 rafter

1×8 fascia (14')

Cap plate

Top plate

FRAMING THE ROOF

The basic shed's roofing plan follows home-construction practices and goes up easily if you approach it one step (and one piece) at a time.

■ **FRAMING INVENTORY:** The roof consists of 2×6 rafters supported by a 2×6 ridge at the top and the cap plates on the wall frame. This design incorporates barge (or verge) rafters, which overhang the gable ends, supported by 2×4 lookouts. A 1×8 fascia hides the exposed rafter tails, and 2×4 collar ties keep the weight of the roof from spreading apart the walls or rafter tails.

■ **SUPPORTING THE RIDGE:** Cut the ridge first and raise it into position with temporary 2×4

braces, as illustrated at the top of the opposite page. Make the supports long enough to place the top of the ridge at the height of the roof. Center the supports on the sidewall and door wall. Make sure each support is straight and plumb, then tack it to both the top plate and the joist. Position the ridge on the support so it extends 10½ inches past the cap plates on both ends. Attach the ridge to the supports.

■ **CUTTING THE RAFTERS:** Cut the first pair of rafters according to the rafter diagram above and test-fit them. When the test rafters fit correctly, use them as templates to cut the remaining rafters. Make the barge rafters for each end ¾ inch longer than the common rafters to cover the end of the ridge board. (See pages 86–89 for more information about laying out and cutting rafters.)

■ **NOTCHING FOR LOOKOUTS:** Notch the four gable-end rafters, as shown in the rafter diagram. Place the notch 4 feet from the top of the rafter to provide sufficient nailing surface for the plywood sheathing.

WASTE NOT...

After installing both the floor and the roof of this 10-foot structure, you'll have some leftover plywood. Instead of throwing it away, cut the pieces into strips and use them for shelves or nailing ledgers for storage.

■ **INSTALLING THE RAFTERS:**
Set each bird's mouth in the rafter
tie on the cap rail and nail it in
place before nailing the rafter to
the ridge. This makes it easier to
position the rafter on the ridge.
Use 16d nails to fasten the rafters
to the ridge. Once you have the
first pair up, the rest fall into place
quickly. Install the main rafters in
opposite pairs. Install the lookouts
and barge rafters last. You can fasten
the collar ties as you go or put them
in after the rafters, whichever you
find easier. Leave the 2×4 ridge
supports in place until you have
sheathed the roof.

■ **FINISHING THE ROOF:** Install
the fascia on the tails of the rafters
next; the edges of the sheathing fit
flush with the front of the fascia.
Bevel the top of the fascia to match
the roof angle and attach it to the
rafter tails with 10d nails. Then
install the plywood sheathing, felt
paper, and shingles. (See pages
90–97 for more information
about roofing.)

INSTALLING THE MAIN ROOF RAFTERS

1. Measure and cut temporary ridge supports and
tack to bottom and top plates on both sidewalls.

2. Tack ridge to supports.

3. Toenail notched gable rafters
to top plate and fasten to ridge.

4. Fasten remaining
rafters.

Notch for
lookout

1× cleats
(optional)

Ridge

4'

8'

2×4 temporary support

NAILING RAFTERS

Face-nail first rafter
through ridge.

Toenail
opposite
rafter.

INSTALLING THE BARGE RAFTERS

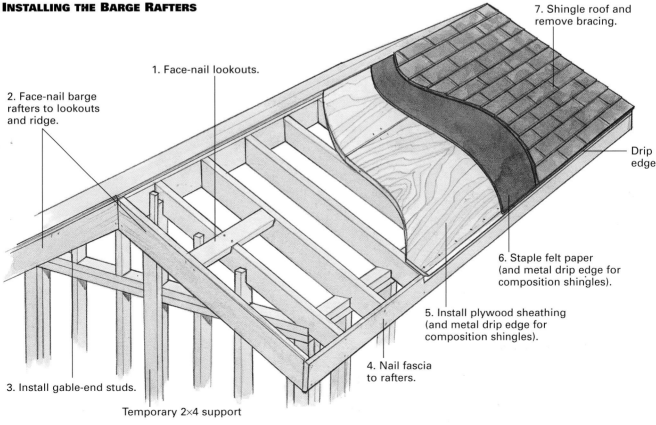

1. Face-nail lookouts.

2. Face-nail barge
rafters to lookouts
and ridge.

3. Install gable-end studs.

Temporary 2×4 support

4. Nail fascia
to rafters.

5. Install plywood sheathing
(and metal drip edge for
composition shingles).

6. Staple felt paper
(and metal drip edge for
composition shingles).

7. Shingle roof and
remove bracing.

Drip
edge

BASIC GARDEN SHED
continued

TRIMMING THE WINDOW

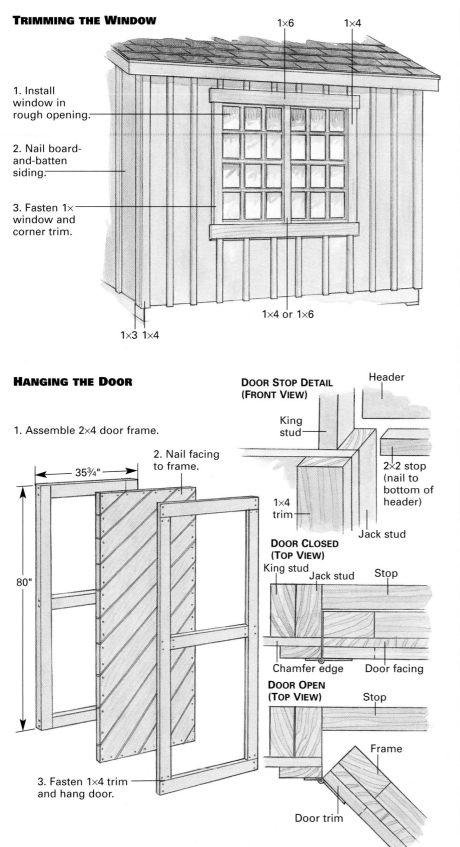

1×6   1×4

1. Install window in rough opening.

2. Nail board-and-batten siding.

3. Fasten 1× window and corner trim.

1×4 or 1×6

1×3 1×4

HANGING THE DOOR

1. Assemble 2×4 door frame.

2. Nail facing to frame.

35¾"

80"

3. Fasten 1×4 trim and hang door.

DOOR STOP DETAIL (FRONT VIEW)

Header

King stud

2×2 stop (nail to bottom of header)

1×4 trim

Jack stud

DOOR CLOSED (TOP VIEW)

King stud   Jack stud   Stop

Chamfer edge   Door facing

DOOR OPEN (TOP VIEW)

Stop

Frame

Door trim

WINDOWS AND SIDING

Whether you install the window or the siding first depends on the type of window. Most windows that have a nailing flange go on before the siding. Cased wood windows are installed after the siding so the casing can be brought flush with the siding. Refer to pages 104–106 for information about windows.

■ **BLOCKING:** Board-and-batten and other vertical sidings require horizontal 2×4 blocking spaced 2 feet on center between the studs. Offset the blocks by 1½ inches so you can face-nail them through the studs. If you don't want to use blocking, you can install sheathing over the walls instead.

Start board-and-batten and other vertical or panel siding flush with the edge of the frame. Plumb the first board with a 4-foot level and check for plumb every three or four boards.

Start installing horizontal siding and shingles at the bottom. Sheathing must be installed for shingles. (See pages 98–101 for more about siding.)

HANGING THE DOOR AND TRIM

The door framing in this design accommodates both the flat-frame styles shown at left and the box-frame style shown on page 21. Flat-frame doors require the 2×2 stop nailed to the bottom of the header, as shown here. If you build a box-frame door and don't want it to be self-trimming, nail a 2×4 to the back of the header and jack studs to act as a stop. Without the stop the door will swing too far into the opening when closed, putting extra stress on the hinges and jack studs.

Trim the shed in the style shown here or install trim of your choice. Using 1×6 trim on tops of windows and doors and extending the horizontal trim beyond the side pieces are ways to add a touch of style to the shed.

ADDING STORAGE AND WORK SPACE

Adequate storage and work space make gardening and yard work more enjoyable. Build a shed that has the type of storage and work space you'll need.

Start by considering the garden tools you have, both hand and power. Organize your racks and shelves according to how frequently you'll use the tools to be stored on them, and find locations that allow easy access. Plan a place that keeps garden chemicals out of children's reach—perhaps on a high shelf supported from the rafters.

Hang long-handle tools on 12d nails driven into 1×4s nailed across the studs. Or, for a more elegant rack, cut ¾-inch dowel rod into 6- to 8-inch lengths and insert them into holes drilled at an angle into 2×4s. To keep the angles consistent, make a jig with a predrilled hole.

Install adjustable shelf tracks to support 1× shelves. Screw and glue a lip along the front edge of each shelf for rigidity and to keep items from slipping off.

Suspended platform shelves transform overhead space into storage areas for light loads, and you can lay light but cumbersome items, from storm windows to long beanpoles, across the collar ties.

BUILDING A WORKBENCH

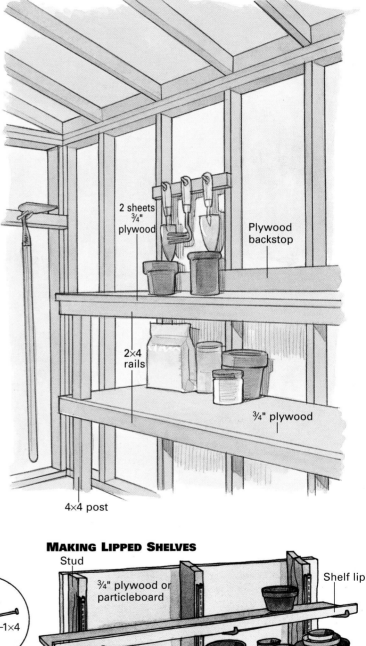

2 sheets ¾" plywood

Plywood backstop

2×4 rails

¾" plywood

4×4 post

INSTALLING HANGING SHELVES

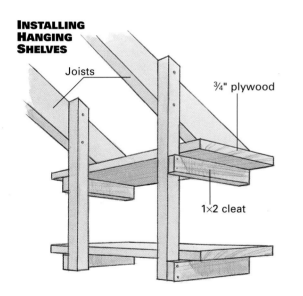

Joists

¾" plywood

1×2 cleat

HANGING TOOL RACKS

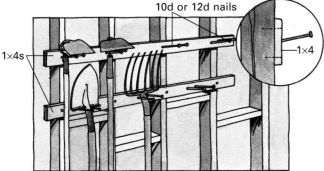

10d or 12d nails

1×4s

1×4

MAKING LIPPED SHELVES

Stud

¾" plywood or particleboard

Shelf lip

Shelf bracket

Shelf bracket   Shelf track

HIPPED-ROOF WORK SHED

This 8×12-foot hipped-roof work shed tucks into the back corner of the yard or fits nicely into a central part of the garden without overwhelming it. Built with cedar or redwood and roofed with shakes, it's perfect for a cottage garden or woodland landscape.

The work shed is essentially a smaller version of the 10×12-foot garden shed described on the previous pages, but its hipped roof gives it a different style. The recessed door frame adds visual mystery to the entrance, a quality enhanced by the peekaboo side windows.

LAYING OUT THE SITE

Use the garden-shed layout frame illustrated on page 23, but set its dimensions at 8×12 feet. Square the corners with a 3-4-5 triangle as shown. Mark the post locations and shed perimeter with spray ground-marking paint.

Remove the frame, dig the postholes, and excavate 4 to 6 inches between the painted lines, depending on your soil conditions. Set the posts and cut them 2 to 3 inches above grade. Then prepare the site with landscape fabric and coarse crushed gravel.

MATERIALS LIST

FOUNDATION, FLOOR, AND WALLS

■ Posts (check local codes)	4×4×8', 4	
■ Joists	2×6×8', 12	
	2×6×12', 2	
■ Floor (¾" plywood)	4×8, 3	
■ Studs, plates	2×4×8', 52	
	2×4×12', 6	
■ Header	2×12×8', 4	
■ Siding	285 sq. ft.	
■ Trim	1×3×8', 4	
	1×4×8', 4	
	1×6×10', 1	

ROOF

■ Area	300 sq. ft.	
■ Shingles	3½ squares	
■ Rafters	2×6×8', 13	
	2×6×12', 6	
■ Roof (½" plywood)	4×8, 9	
■ Fascia	1×8×8', 4	
	1×8×12', 2	

Overlap the fabric edges by 10 to 12 inches. When placing the gravel, dump it from a wheelbarrow in several small piles per square yard. Avoid large piles of gravel—it's hard to move and you want to make this part of the task as easy as possible. Move the piles with a round-nose shovel and level it with the back of a garden rake. (For more on site preparation and foundation work, see pages 80–81.)

FRAMING THE FLOOR

Build the work shed floor frame from 2×6 treated lumber that's rated for ground contact.

■ **ASSEMBLE THE JOISTS:** Mark the rim joists at 16 inches on center for the joist hangers and toenail the perimeter box to the posts. Check the frame for square before you drive the nails home. To do so, measure the diagonals; the corners are square if the diagonals are equal. Face-nail the corners and strengthen them with angle brackets. Attach the joist hangers, then place the joists in the hangers.

WORK SHED (PERSPECTIVE VIEW)

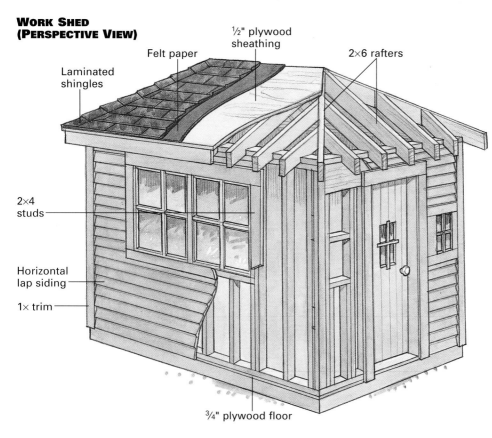

Laminated shingles

Felt paper

½" plywood sheathing

2×6 rafters

2×4 studs

Horizontal lap siding

1× trim

¾" plywood floor

REAR WALL FRAMING PLAN

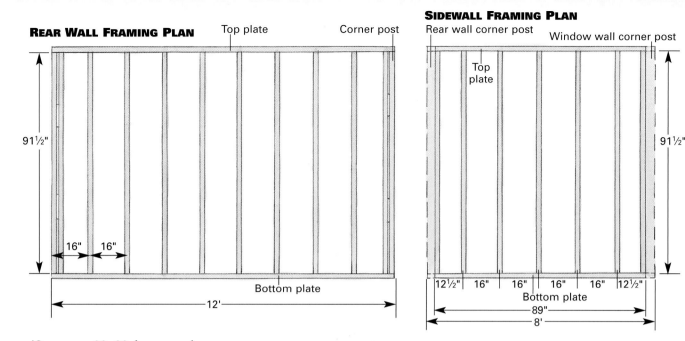

Top plate

Corner post

91½"

16"   16"

Bottom plate

12'

SIDEWALL FRAMING PLAN

Rear wall corner post

Window wall corner post

Top plate

91½"

12½" 16" 16" 16" 16" 12½"

Bottom plate

89"

8'

(See pages 82–83 for more about floor framing.)

■ **COVER THE FLOOR:** Install the plywood floor. This plan is built in 4-foot increments, so you can cover it with three sheets of plywood without waste. Offset the joints, leaving ⅛ inch between them. Nail them with 10d nails, as shown on page 23. If the plywood overhangs the framing, trim the excess with a circular saw. Cutting the flooring to match the squared frame ensures that the wall framing and everything above it will be square. It's easier to trim the flooring than it is to force a reluctant wall into square.

FRAMING THE WALLS

Refer to the framing plans on this page and follow the techniques described on pages 24–25 to preassemble the walls. The door wall for this shed uses 2×6 jack studs instead of 2×4s—the extra width creates the doorway recess. If you don't want the recess, use 2×4 jack studs.

■ **START WITH A LONG WALL:** Start with one of the long walls and work around the perimeter of the structure. Enlist the aid of a helper to raise the walls in place. Brace them to the floor with 1×3 boards and keep them square with 1×3 diagonal braces. Once the walls are up and braced, tie the corners together with 2×4 cap plates that overlap the adjacent walls, as shown at the bottom of page 25. Mark the cap plates for the rafter centers and attach rafter ties. (See pages 84–85 for more about building walls.)

WINDOW WALL FRAMING PLAN

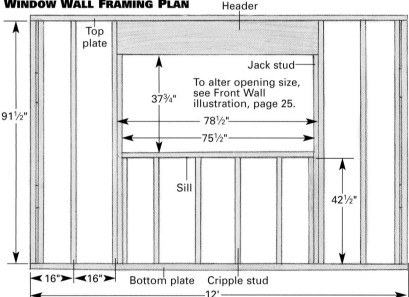

Header

Top plate

Jack stud

To alter opening size, see Front Wall illustration, page 25.

37¾"

78½"

75½"

91½"

42½"

Sill

16"   16"   Bottom plate   Cripple stud

12'

DOOR WALL FRAMING PLAN

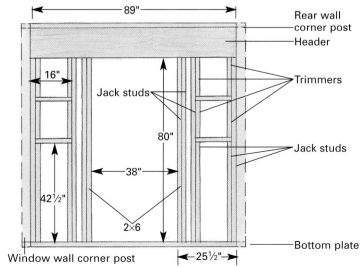

89"

Rear wall corner post

Header

16"

Jack studs

Trimmers

80"

Jack studs

38"

42½"

2×6

Window wall corner post

25½"

Bottom plate

HIPPED-ROOF WORK SHED
continued

as they might appear. Hipped-roof rafters, however, do require careful layout.

AN INTRODUCTION TO THE HIPPED ROOF

A hipped roof has sloping sides and sloping ends. Study the roof framing plan on this page before you begin to build it. Although hipped roofs are somewhat more complicated than gable roofs, they aren't as difficult to build

CUTTING THE RAFTERS

The dimensions in the rafter diagrams are for the roof shown, so you won't have to make any framing-square computations unless you change the building size or roof pitch. (See pages 86–89 for more about laying out and cutting rafters.)

■ RIDGE RAFTERS:
The ridge (or end) rafters are ¾ inch shorter than the common rafters.

■ HIP RAFTERS:
Bevel the end of the hip rafters 45 degrees on each side to fit into the joint between the ridge rafter and the common rafter. This compound miter is easier to cut on a power miter saw. Turn the saw table to 45 degrees and the bevel gauge to the angle of the roof that matches the pitch—26.5 degrees for the 6/12 roof shown here. (See the table on page 88 for other roof angles).

Chamfer the hip rafters or deepen the bird's-mouth cut as needed to bring the top edge into the plane of the common rafters (see page 89).

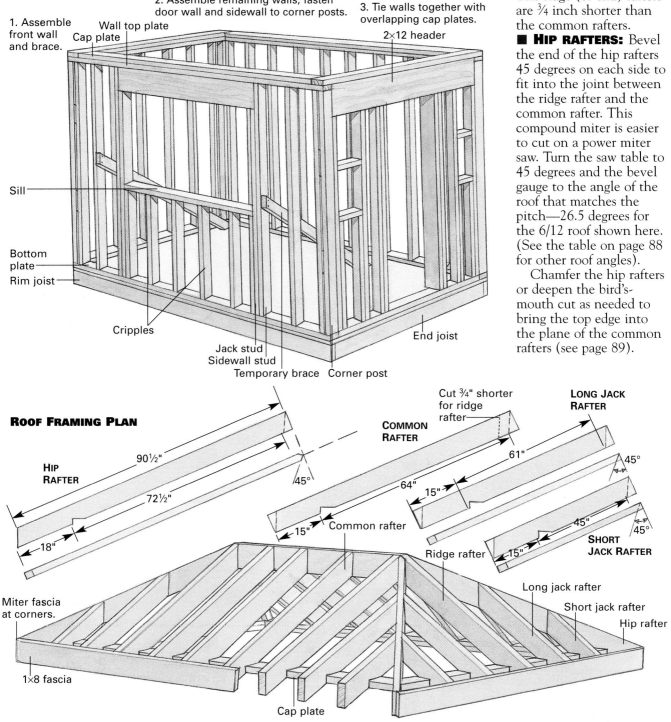

ERECTING THE WALLS

1. Assemble front wall and brace.
2. Assemble remaining walls; fasten door wall and sidewall to corner posts.
3. Tie walls together with overlapping cap plates.

Wall top plate
Cap plate
2×12 header
Sill
Bottom plate
Rim joist
Cripples
End joist
Jack stud
Sidewall stud
Temporary brace
Corner post

ROOF FRAMING PLAN

HIP RAFTER
90½"
72½"
18"
45°

COMMON RAFTER
64"
15"
Common rafter
Cut ¾" shorter for ridge rafter
61"
15"
Ridge rafter

LONG JACK RAFTER
45°
45"
45°

SHORT JACK RAFTER
15"
45°

Long jack rafter
Short jack rafter
Hip rafter

Miter fascia at corners.
1×8 fascia
Cap plate

■ **JACK RAFTERS:** Bevel the jack rafters at 45 degrees on a power miter saw. The bevels are left-hand on one side and right-hand on the other. Label each piece as you cut it to avoid confusion.

RAISING THE ROOF

When it comes to hipped-roof framing, getting the ridge in the correct place at the start is critical.

■ Cut a temporary support long enough to raise the ridge to its correct height and fasten it 1½ inches to one side of the ridge's midpoint.

■ Nail the middle common rafters to the midpoint of the ridge, and hoist the assembly into place.

■ Drop the bird's mouths into the rafter ties and nail the rafters to the cap plates. Then plumb the 2×4 support and tack it to the floor.

■ Stabilize the support with another 2×4 tacked to the end wall. Then attach the ridge rafters and the remaining rafters. Leave the braces in place until you have sheathed three roof sections.

FINISHING THE ROOF

Bevel the top edge of the fascia to the angle of the roof, and install the fascia before sheathing the roof. Start the sheathing at the front edge of the fascia and fasten the sections with 10d nails. Complete each roof section with the center sheet, then the one above it, chalking a line at the cutoffs and cutting away the excess with your circular saw. Then go back and use the excess to fill in the remaining spaces. Offset the sheathing joints, and space the sheets ⅛ inch apart. Staple felt paper, and shingle the roof. (See pages 90–97 for more information.)

HANGING THE DOOR

The door frame accommodates a standard prehung door but uses a 2×6 jack stud to recess it into the wall. Install the door with the jamb flush at the rear edge of the jack stud. Install trim in the recess, leaving a ¼-inch reveal, as shown at right. To cover the gap above the door and the jack stud, rip a 2×4 to 2 inches and face-nail it to the top of the jack stud.

INSTALLING THE FIRST RAFTERS

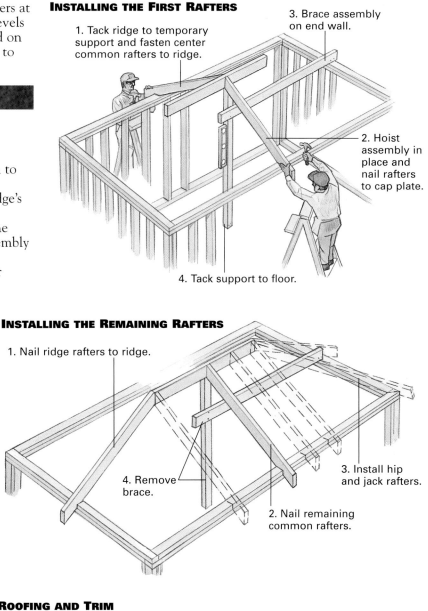

3. Brace assembly on end wall.

1. Tack ridge to temporary support and fasten center common rafters to ridge.

2. Hoist assembly in place and nail rafters to cap plate.

4. Tack support to floor.

INSTALLING THE REMAINING RAFTERS

1. Nail ridge rafters to ridge.

4. Remove brace.

3. Install hip and jack rafters.

2. Nail remaining common rafters.

ROOFING AND TRIM

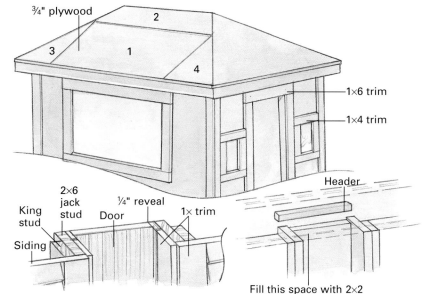

¾" plywood

1×6 trim

1×4 trim

2×6 jack stud

King stud

Siding

Door

¼" reveal

1× trim

Header

Fill this space with 2×2

POTTING SHED

This potting shed is similar to the work shed shown on pages 30–33, but it has a gable roof and a portico that extends over the entry. The 4×4 posts that support the portico, clean trim lines, and narrow windows create a classic look suitable for a formal landscape. On the other hand, it provides a pleasant contrast in an informal cottage garden.

PORTICO PRELIMINARIES

Think of the portico as a small room without walls. The portico roof meets the main roof the way a dormer would. The shed in effect has two perpendicular gable roofs.

BUILDING THE MAIN FLOOR

The addition of the portico makes laying out this shed a little trickier than a four-sided structure. Before you lay out the portico, use the layout frame on page 23 to prepare the site for an 8×12 structure. Set the posts, cut them, and build the floor frame complete with flooring, as described on page 23. The floor framing provides a reference point for establishing the portico dimensions. (See pages 82–83 for more about floor framing.)

ADDING THE PORTICO

Start by marking the center at the front of the main floor. Tack mason's lines to the rim joist 24 inches from each side of the center.

■ **LOCATING THE POSTS:** Stretch the lines perpendicular to the rim joist to triangulated stakes about 3 feet from the

POTTING SHED (PERSPECTIVE VIEW)

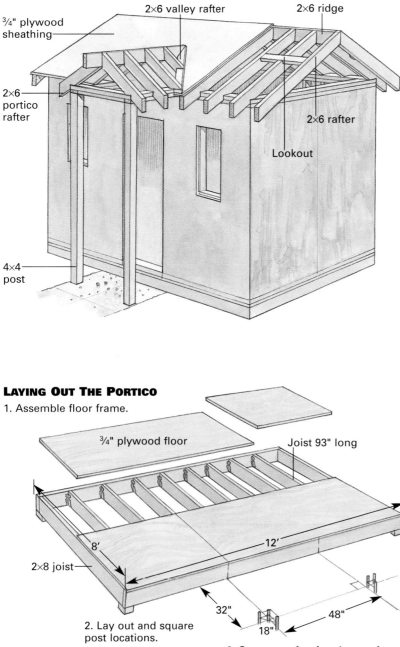

¾" plywood sheathing

2×6 valley rafter

2×6 ridge

2×6 portico rafter

2×6 rafter

Lookout

4×4 post

LAYING OUT THE PORTICO

1. Assemble floor frame.

¾" plywood floor

Joist 93" long

2×8 joist

8'

12'

32"

18"

48"

2. Lay out and square post locations.

3. Set posts after framing roof.

MATERIALS LIST

FOUNDATION, FLOOR, AND WALLS

■ Posts (check local codes)		4×4×8', 4
		4×4×12', 2
■ Joists		2×8×8', 10
		2×8×12', 2
■ Floor (¾" plywood)		4×8, 3
■ Studs, plates		2×4×8', 66
		2×4×12', 6
■ Header		2×12×8', 2
■ Siding		350 sq. ft.
■ Trim		1×3×8', 8
		1×4×8', 6
		1×6×8', 2

ROOF

■ Area		300 sq. ft.
■ Shingles		3½ squares
■ Rafters		2×6×10', 4
		2×6×14', 13
■ Roof (½" plywood)		4×8, 10
■ Fascia		1×8, 30'

rim joist. Because the dimensions of the portico are small, square the corners with a scaled-down version of the 3-4-5 triangle. Use 18, 24, and 30 inches as your marks, and adjust the stakes to locate the posts where shown in the illustration at left.

■ **SETTING THE POSTS:** Dig the postholes, pour 3 to 4 inches of dry concrete mix into the bottom, and insert the posts. Make sure the posts are more than 8 feet tall. If you removed the lines to dig the holes, reset them and line up the edges of the post with the intersection. Tamp the earth with a 2×4, keeping the post plumbed on two adjacent sides. Don't cut the posts until the walls are in place.

ERECTING THE WALLS

Follow the framing plans for the rear wall and sidewalls shown for the work shed walls on page 31. Build two sidewalls, but not the door wall, for the work shed. Construct the front wall according to the framing diagram at right.

■ **BUILDING THE MAIN WALLS:** Assemble the walls and raise them on the floor frame, as discussed on page 31. Tie the corners with cap plates and install rafter ties, then plumb. (See pages 84–85 for more about building walls.)

FRONT WALL FRAMING PLAN

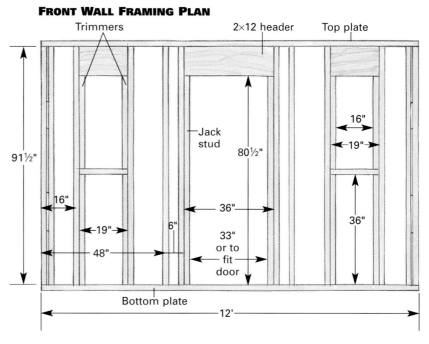

ERECTING THE WALLS

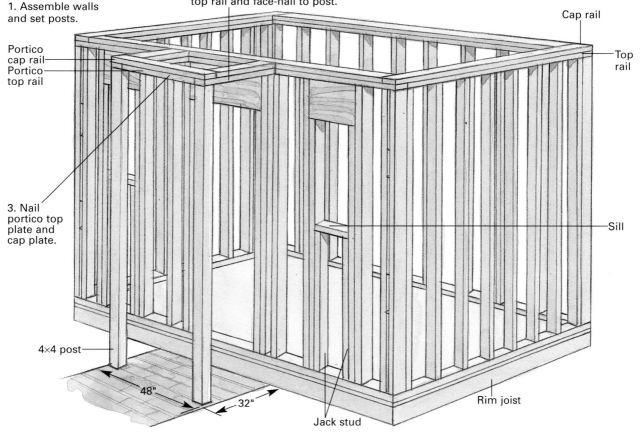

POTTING SHED
continued

ROOF FRAMING PLAN

RAFTER DIAGRAM

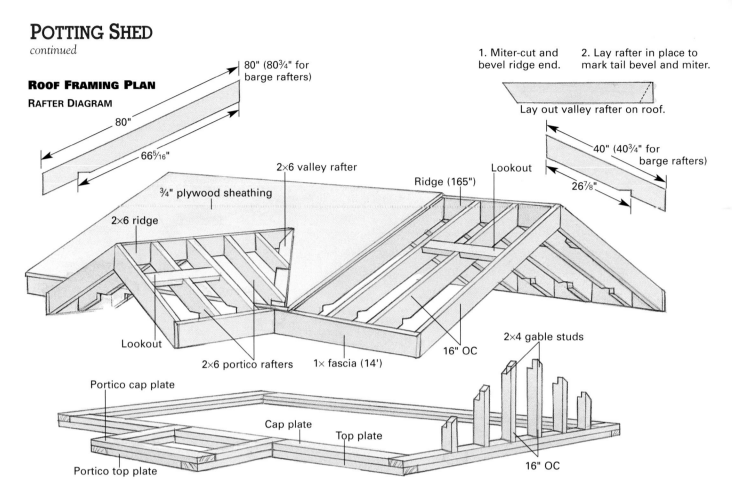

1. Miter-cut and bevel ridge end.

2. Lay rafter in place to mark tail bevel and miter.

Lay out valley rafter on roof.

80" (80¾" for barge rafters)

80"

66⁵⁄₁₆"

2×6 valley rafter

¾" plywood sheathing

Ridge (165")

Lookout

40" (40¾" for barge rafters)

26⅞"

2×6 ridge

2×4 gable studs

Lookout

2×6 portico rafters

1× fascia (14')

16" OC

Portico cap plate

Cap plate

Top plate

Portico top plate

16" OC

FRAMING THE PORTICO ROOF

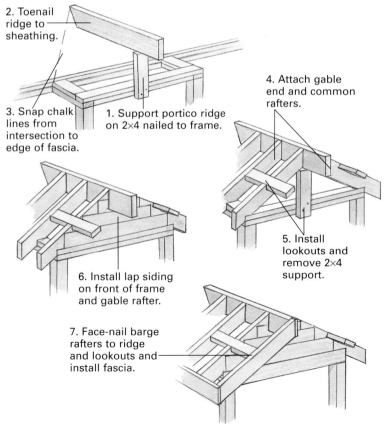

2. Toenail ridge to sheathing.

3. Snap chalk lines from intersection to edge of fascia.

1. Support portico ridge on 2×4 nailed to frame.

4. Attach gable end and common rafters.

5. Install lookouts and remove 2×4 support.

6. Install lap siding on front of frame and gable rafter.

7. Face-nail barge rafters to ridge and lookouts and install fascia.

■ **LINING UP THE PORTICO PLATES:**
To line up the portico plates exactly with the posts, first cut the posts level with the bottom of the top plate. Use a mason's line and line level to mark the post height, and cut each one with a reciprocating saw.

■ **PORTICO TOP PLATES:** Place a 2×4 on top of one post and square it to the main top plate with a framing square. Mark the main top plate at the intersection of the 2×4, cut it to length, and toenail it to the top plate. Face-nail the portico top plate to the top of the post and repeat the process on the other side. Measure the distance between the posts, and toenail the front portico top plate level with the side plates.

■ **PORTICO CAP PLATE:** Extend the portico top-plate lines to the front-wall cap plate. Cut out the 3½-inch section between the lines to allow the portico cap plate to lie on the front-wall top plate. Nail the portico cap plates, as shown at left.

FRAMING THE ROOF

Build the main roof using the procedures described on pages 26–27 and 86–89. Bevel and install the fascias.

■ **INSTALLING THE FIRST PORTICO RAFTERS:** Cut the portico rafters and lookouts. Support the portico ridge and gable-end rafters with a 2×4 nailed to the portico plates. Nail the ridge to the sheathing, centered on the front wall. Snap chalk lines from the intersection of the ridge down to the intersection of the portico plates and the outer edge of the fascia. Lay out the valley rafters using the chalk lines.

■ **INSTALLING THE REMAINING RAFTERS:** Fasten the remaining portico rafters to the ridge and sheathing, keeping the rafter tails lined up on the chalk line. Nail the lookouts and install siding on the front of the portico. Then face-nail the portico barge rafters and fascia.

■ **FINISHING THE ROOF:** Shingle the roof following the procedures shown for shingling a dormer or roof extension on pages 93–95. Start by sheathing the portico and stapling felt paper, creating a valley as shown on page 91. Shingle the roof with composition shingles or the material of your choice. All roofing except untreated wood shingles can be installed over plywood.

INSTALLING THE SIDING

For horizontal lap siding, install a spacer or molding at the bottom of the first course, as shown on page 100. Use a story pole (page 101) to space the siding, beginning on the front wall and transferring the lines around the remainder of the building. If you start on one of the sidewalls, the lines probably won't correspond to the top and bottom of the doorway and windows. Nail the siding into the studs with 8d nails, then add trim.

HANGING THE DOOR

The rough opening and door frame is designed to accommodate a standard 32-inch prehung exterior door. (See page 102 for information about installing doors.)

You may not be able to find the exact door illustrated, but any full-view steel (or wood) door with a center pane of glass will work. Most models come with snap-in muntins that allow you to create the pattern of your choice.

You can install a solid panel door and still achieve the same overall design effect, but you'll lose the interior light, making the shed less inviting for potting.

If you install a solid door, consider electrifying the shed or installing additional windows or skylights. This is a decision you should make during the planning stage of your project. It's possible to add windows to existing walls but much easier to install them in framing that was designed for them.

TRIMMING DETAILS

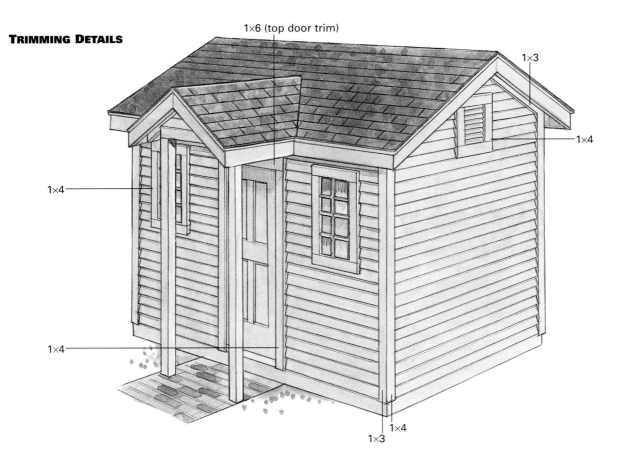

1×6 (top door trim)

1×3

1×4

1×4

1×4

1×4

1×3

DESIGNING GAZEBOS

Building a gazebo looks complicated because it has more than four sides, but construction shouldn't be a challenge. The 2×6 layout frame employed in this design dispenses with complicated geometry and computations, and since it's adjustable, you can adapt it to any size.

The plans in this book use 2×4 corner studs instead of posts, which minimizes the number of angle cuts; allows you to install a variety of gussets, friezes, sidings, and enclosures; and provides wiring channels for lights, fans, and speakers. This design also allows you to test-fit the rafters at ground level, making construction significantly easier—you can fit the rafters, adjust the pitch and overhang, and check the height before hoisting the framing on a ladder.

The basic frame shown on pages 42–49 can be left open or enclosed. If you decide to build a screened or closed design, read the appropriate pages to familiarize yourself with the changes required to add the cupola, screens, or siding. If you change the design, make scaled drawings before you begin construction.

Use treated lumber rated for ground contact for the posts and floor frame; use redwood, cedar, or treated lumber for the rest of the structure. Small variations in dimensions often occur in carpentry projects, so verify measurements and test-fit parts before you cut multiple pieces.

PERSPECTIVE VIEW

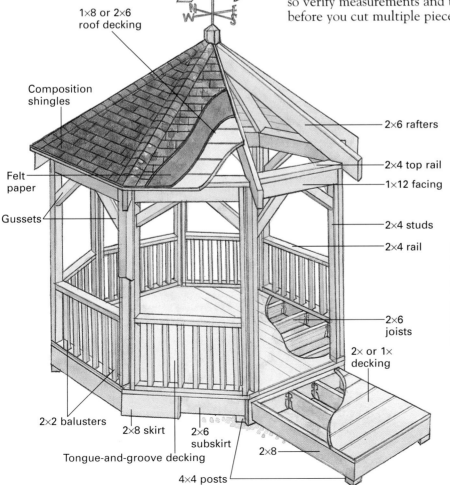

1×8 or 2×6 roof decking

Composition shingles

Felt paper

Gussets

2×2 balusters

2×8 skirt

2×6 subskirt

Tongue-and-groove decking

4×4 posts

2×8

2×6 rafters

2×4 top rail

1×12 facing

2×4 studs

2×4 rail

2×6 joists

2× or 1× decking

DRESSING UP THE EDGES

Square lumber edges look just fine inside a garden shed. After all, the interior of a shed is primarily functional. Gazebos, however, are all about style. Dress up the edges of exposed framing and trim with chamfered, rounded, or molded edges made with a router bit. This added touch enhances your gazebo's custom-built look.

SITE LAYOUT AND POST SETTING

LAYOUT FRAME FOR GAZEBO

Fasten corners and diagonals with 3" decking screws.

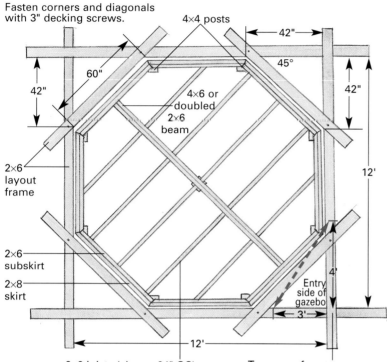

4×4 posts

42"

45°

60"

42"

42"

4×6 or doubled 2×6 beam

12'

2×6 layout frame

2×6 subskirt

2×8 skirt

4'

Entry side of gazebo

3'

12'

2×6 joists (shown 24" OC)
(Install nine joists for 16" OC.)

To square frame corners, mark one side 3' and one 4' from the corner. Adjust the angle until distance between marks (dotted red line) is 5'.

The integrity of any structure depends on its foundation. Lay out the site accurately and set the posts solidly to minimize difficulties during later construction. The layout frame shown at left ensures accurate post placement.

LAYING OUT THE SITE

Before you build the layout frame, level the site. Remove rocks, grade down high spots, and mow the grass to about 1 inch. Prop the frame on bricks or blocks where there are minor inconsistencies in the grade. If the ground falls away sharply, you'll have to build temporary supports.

The 12-foot floor plan shown has facets of about 60 inches. The facet length increases or decreases about 5 inches for every 1 foot change in gazebo diameter.

INSTALLING THE DIAGONALS

Square the corners using the 3-4-5 triangle method, as shown in the illustration at left. Measure from the inside corner of the frame. Using an 8-foot board for each diagonal, mark

LAYING OUT THE SITE AND SETTING THE POSTS

1. Set 2×6 layout frame and stake corners.

2. Fasten corners of frame.

3. Square corners with 3-4-5 triangle and install diagonals securely.

4. Locate center post where midpoints of sides intersect.

5. Mark post locations.

6. Dig postholes.

7. Set posts with template.

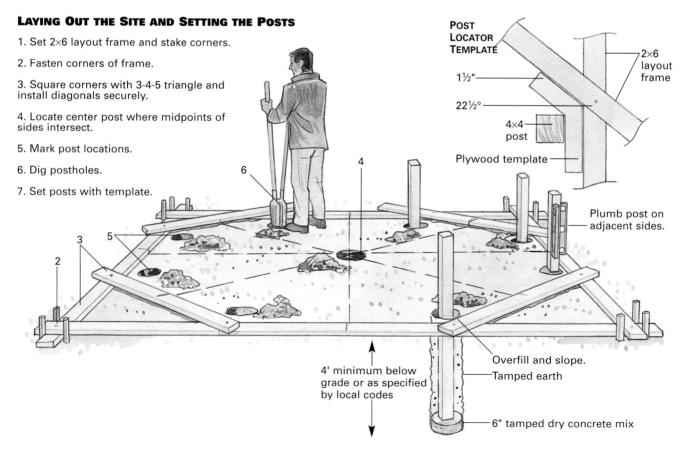

POST LOCATOR TEMPLATE

1½"

22½°

4×4 post

Plywood template

2×6 layout frame

Plumb post on adjacent sides.

6

4

5

3

2

4' minimum below grade or as specified by local codes

Overfill and slope.

Tamped earth

6" tamped dry concrete mix

DO YOU NEED A STEP?

A 2×6 floor structure at ground level with ¾-inch hardwood decking results in a finished floor height of about 7 inches. Most codes do not require a step or entry landing for this height. If you want to add a step for easier entry or for appearance, see "Building a Step" on page 53.

If you install thicker decking or modify the design so the floor is more than 7½ inches off the ground, you may not have a choice—local codes may require that a step be built.

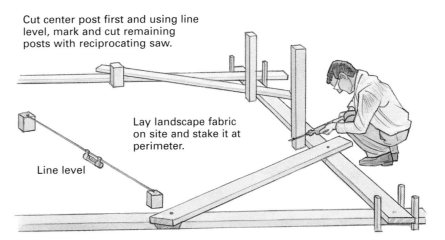

Cut center post first and using line level, mark and cut remaining posts with reciprocating saw.

Lay landscape fabric on site and stake it at perimeter.

Line level

a 5-foot length in the middle (18 inches from each end).

Mark each frame member 42 inches from the corner. Lay the diagonal on the frame and align the 5-foot marks on the diagonal with the marks on the frame sides. Fasten the diagonal to the frame with two 3-inch decking screws at each overlap.

MATERIALS LIST

FOUNDATION, FLOOR, AND WALLS

Posts	4×4×10', 5	
Joists	2×6×12', 5	
	2×6×10', 2	
Subskirt	2×6×12', 4	
Skirt	2×8×12', 4	
■ Deck	2×6×12', 18	
	2×6×10', 20	
Studs, plates	2×4×8', 4	
	2×4×10', 20	
Header trim	1×12×12', 8	
Sill	2×6×12', 4	
■ Rail support	2×4×10', 4	
■ Balusters	2×2, 75'	

ROOF

Area	220 square feet	
Shingles	2½ squares	
Rafters	2×6×10', 8	
■ Facing	1×12×12', 4	
Roof boards	1×8×10', 35	
or tongue-and-groove	2×6×10', 55	
OSB or plywood	4×8, 8	
Trim	1×6×12', 12	

MARKING THE CENTER POST

The center post and beam keep the floor from flexing under a load. Locate the center post at the intersection of lines tied at the midpoints of the sides. Mark all post locations with spray marking paint.

SETTING THE POSTS

Set each post square to the frame and 1½ inches from it using the locator template shown on the opposite page. With the skirt in place, the floor will be 12 feet wide.

Set each post into about 2 inches of dry concrete mix at the bottom of the hole. The concrete will solidify with ground moisture. Hold the post against the template and tamp the soil around it with a 2×4. Plumb the post on adjacent sides as you go.

CUTTING THE POSTS

To cut the posts' ends to the same height, use a line level on a taut mason's line, as shown in the illustration above. Draw guidelines on the post before cutting to ensure a square cut.

BUILDING A SLAB FLOOR

Although the gazebo illustrated in the plans on these pages employs a wood frame floor, you can use the same layout methods to install an octagonal concrete slab.

Lay out the site and mark the perimeter with spray marking paint. Remove the layout frame, excavate, build forms, and pour a concrete slab using the techniques shown on pages 80–83.

FRAMING THE FLOOR

The floor framing comprises a central beam and joists that are attached to 2×6 subskirt. The subskirt is then toenailed to the post tops. A 2×8 skirt covers the subskirt. The floor is covered with 1×6 or 2×6 hardwood decking.

INSTALLING THE SUBSKIRT

Boards for the subskirt are alternately cut at 45 degrees and 90 degrees, as shown in the illustration below. Measure between the corners of two posts for the first board A.

Install the subskirt one board at a time, so you can fit each board to the actual post layout. Toenail the boards to the post tops with 10d spiral nails, and snug the miters together with 8d nails. After installing the first two boards, measure from the long corners of the subskirt.

CENTER BEAM AND JOISTS

The double 2×6 beam extends from the entry opening to the opposite facet, placing the decking perpendicular to the entry opening. If you want to install the decking with a different orientation, reposition the beam and joists. Draw the alterations on a scaled drawing before beginning construction.

Install the beam with a double joist hanger. Mark the joist locations on the beam and subskirt (16 inches on center for 1× decking, 24 inches on center for 2× decking). Some joists are miter-cut at 45 degrees on one end to meet the angled subskirt.

SKIRTING AND FLOORING

Cut the skirt boards with 22½-degree miters and face-nail them to the subskirt with 10d rust-resistant finishing nails. Keep the top edge flush with the subskirt. Apply construction adhesive to the ends, and snug the miters with 8d nails.

SUBSKIRT AND SKIRT DIMENSIONS

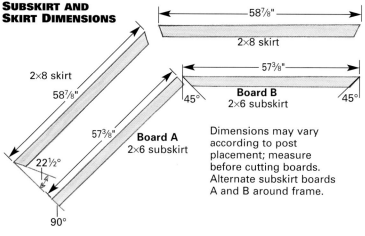

58⅞"
2×8 skirt

2×8 skirt
58⅞"

57⅜"
Board B
2×6 subskirt
45°   45°

57⅜"   **Board A**
2×6 subskirt

22½°

90°

Dimensions may vary according to post placement; measure before cutting boards. Alternate subskirt boards A and B around frame.

INSTALLING THE SUBSKIRT

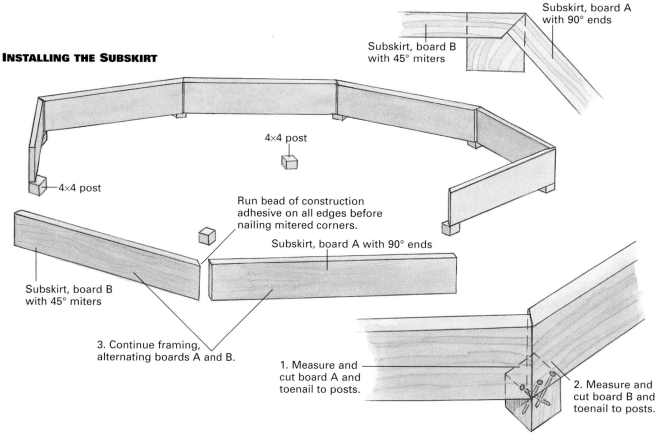

Subskirt, board A with 90° ends

Subskirt, board B with 45° miters

4×4 post

4×4 post

Run bead of construction adhesive on all edges before nailing mitered corners.

Subskirt, board A with 90° ends

Subskirt, board B with 45° miters

3. Continue framing, alternating boards A and B.

1. Measure and cut board A and toenail to posts.

2. Measure and cut board B and toenail to posts.

To keep insects out of a screened gazebo, staple fiberglass screening on top of the joists, overlapping the edges by 4 inches.

Start laying decking boards in the center of the doorway and work to the edges. Nail the flooring with 10d rust-resistant finishing nails. Let the ends run wild over the edge. Lay the boards for the last few courses in place but do not fasten them. To avoid narrow edge boards, rip the last boards to equal widths that fill the remaining space.

To cut the edges flush, measure under the decking to the skirt on each face. Mark the skirt position on the decking and snap a chalk line between the marks. Trim the decking along the lines with a circular saw, taking care not to cut into the skirt.

INSTALLING THE BEAM AND JOISTS

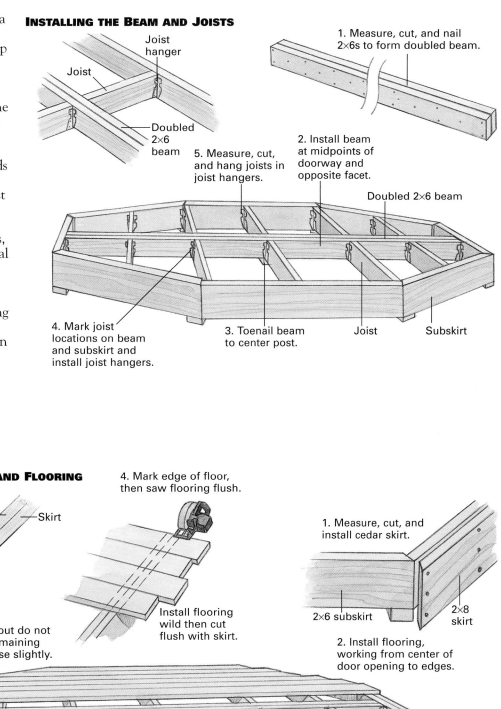

Joist hanger

Joist

Doubled 2×6 beam

1. Measure, cut, and nail 2×6s to form doubled beam.

2. Install beam at midpoints of doorway and opposite facet.

Doubled 2×6 beam

5. Measure, cut, and hang joists in joist hangers.

4. Mark joist locations on beam and subskirt and install joist hangers.

3. Toenail beam to center post.

Joist

Subskirt

INSTALLING THE SKIRT AND FLOORING

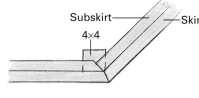

Subskirt — Skirt

4×4

4. Mark edge of floor, then saw flooring flush.

Install flooring wild then cut flush with skirt.

1. Measure, cut, and install cedar skirt.

2×6 subskirt

2×8 skirt

2. Install flooring, working from center of door opening to edges.

3. Lay the last four courses but do not fasten them. Average the remaining distance and trim each course slightly.

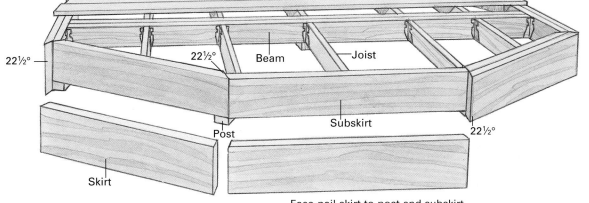

$22\frac{1}{2}°$

$22\frac{1}{2}°$

Beam

Joist

$22\frac{1}{2}°$

Post

Subskirt

Skirt

Face-nail skirt to post and subskirt.

TEST-FITTING THE RAFTERS

Because the floor and top-plate dimensions are the same, you can lay out, cut, and test-fit the rafters on the floor. This means you won't have to erect temporary rafter supports or climb up and down ladders to get the fit right.

The 2×6 rafters are strong enough to span the structures shown on these pages. If you plan to build a larger structure, consult a span table to see if you'll need larger rafters.

This method for test-fitting the rafters works for a closed roof, with or without a cupola. If you're building a gazebo with a cupola, refer to pages 50–52.

CUTTING THE ROOF CENTER POST

Cut the roof center post from a straight length of 4×4 stock of the same species as the other visible parts of the structure. The lengths shown accommodate any roof pitch and can be trimmed on the inside after you've tested the rafters.

Cutting the 4×4 as shown results in an octagon with 1½-inch faces—the thickness of the rafters. Mark the lines precisely with a sharp pencil and straightedge. Cut off the corners on a table saw.

Chamfer the post top to the angle of the pitch of the roof (see table, page 88). Mark the angle with a protractor—a plastic one works just fine.

TOP PLATE AND TEST RAFTERS

Measure the length of the top plates along the edges of the floor. Miter-cut the plate ends 22½ degrees. Cut a top plate for each side, and mark the plates for position. Tack the plates along the floor edge, as shown on the opposite page.

Snap chalk lines between the midpoints of opposite faces. Mark the center of the floor (also the center of the roof peak) where the lines intersect. Then measure from an outside corner to the center to find the length of the rafter run.

Determine the rafter length for your roof pitch using the rafter scales on the framing square (see page 88). Rafter lengths for three roof pitches on a 12-foot gazebo are shown in the illustration below. Cut the rafters 18 to 24 inches longer than the calculated length to allow for the tails. Make the bird's-mouth

CENTER POST DIMENSIONS

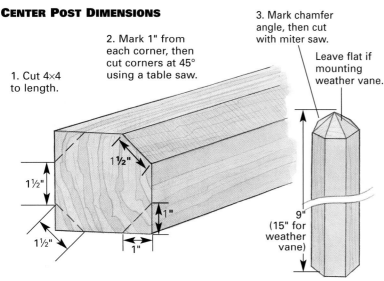

1. Cut 4×4 to length.

2. Mark 1" from each corner, then cut corners at 45° using a table saw.

3. Mark chamfer angle, then cut with miter saw.

Leave flat if mounting weather vane.

9" (15" for weather vane)

1½" 1½" 1½" 1" 1"

LAYING OUT A RAFTER

1. Using framing square, compute length of rafter (from top of test plumb cut to corner of bird's mouth) for run and pitch of roof.

2. Set framing square for pitch (here, 6/12), mark cut lines, and cut rafter to length, leaving an 18–24" tail for overhang.

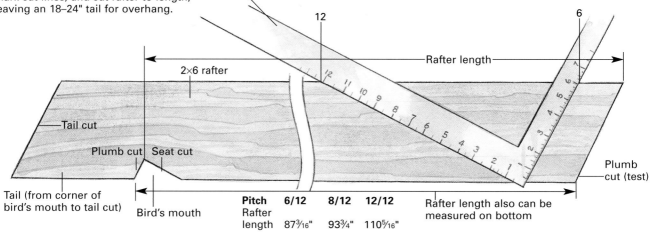

2×6 rafter

12   6

Rafter length

Tail cut

Plumb cut   Seat cut

Plumb cut (test)

Tail (from corner of bird's mouth to tail cut)

Bird's mouth

Rafter length also can be measured on bottom

Pitch	6/12	8/12	12/12
Rafter length	87³⁄₁₆"	93¾"	110⁵⁄₁₆"

cut and test plumb cut on two rafters. Don't make the final plumb cut or tail cut or cut any more rafters until you have tested the rafters as described below.

TESTING THE FIRST RAFTERS

Make a temporary support from a 2×4 and two thicknesses of ¾-inch plywood to test the rafters. Doubling the plywood raises the 2×4 to the same height as the top plate. Cut the 2×4 to the height of the roof above the top plate, as shown at right. Screw two rafters to the support as illustrated.

Center the support on the decking, and place the rafters on opposite corners. If you don't like the way the pitch looks, or if the rafters don't fit, recut them. When the rafters fit properly, cut the final plumb cut 1¾ inches back from the first one to allow for the thickness of the center post. Trim the tail cut to the correct overhang. Lay out and cut the other rafters, using the test rafters as a pattern.

REMAINING RAFTERS AND ROOF

Shorten the 2×4 temporary support so you can tack the roof center post to it at the height of the roof. Then tack opposing pairs of rafters to the faces of the center post, keeping the post plumb.

Line up the rafters on the corners and recut any that need adjusting. Then cut the roof sheathing pieces to fit, but don't fasten them.

Before you disassemble the rafters and center post, number the rafters and roofing sections so you can put them up in the same order. Mark the center post where it meets the bottoms of the rafters. Take apart the assembly, and trim the post to the mark.

Then recut all the bird's-mouth plumb cuts ¾ inch longer so the 1× facing can slide into place on the face of the wall later.

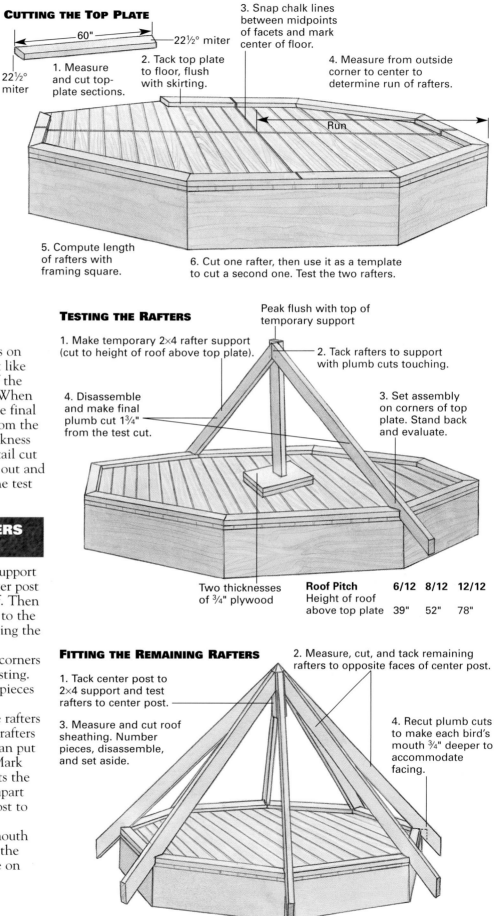

CUTTING THE TOP PLATE

60"

22½° miter

22½° miter

1. Measure and cut top-plate sections.

2. Tack top plate to floor, flush with skirting.

3. Snap chalk lines between midpoints of facets and mark center of floor.

4. Measure from outside corner to center to determine run of rafters.

Run

5. Compute length of rafters with framing square.

6. Cut one rafter, then use it as a template to cut a second one. Test the two rafters.

TESTING THE RAFTERS

Peak flush with top of temporary support

1. Make temporary 2×4 rafter support (cut to height of roof above top plate).

2. Tack rafters to support with plumb cuts touching.

3. Set assembly on corners of top plate. Stand back and evaluate.

4. Disassemble and make final plumb cut 1¾" from the test cut.

Two thicknesses of ¾" plywood

Roof Pitch	6/12	8/12	12/12
Height of roof above top plate	39"	52"	78"

FITTING THE REMAINING RAFTERS

1. Tack center post to 2×4 support and test rafters to center post.

2. Measure, cut, and tack remaining rafters to opposite faces of center post.

3. Measure and cut roof sheathing. Number pieces, disassemble, and set aside.

4. Recut plumb cuts to make each bird's mouth ¾" deeper to accommodate facing.

BUILDING THE WALLS

The roof load rests on the studs, not the wall top plates, so walls are built with flat 2×4 headers above the openings instead of doubled 2× stock. This framing eliminates the extra expense of a doubled header and provides space to run wiring. The 1×12 facing provides lateral strength and keeps the header from sagging.

GAZEBO WALL FRAMING

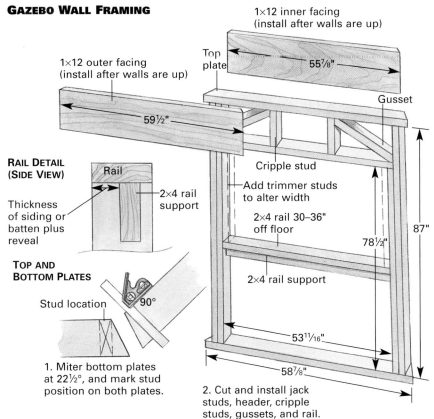

1×12 outer facing (install after walls are up)

59½"

1×12 inner facing (install after walls are up)

Top plate

55⅞"

Gusset

Cripple stud

Add trimmer studs to alter width

2×4 rail 30–36" off floor

2×4 rail support

87"

78½"

53¹¹⁄₁₆"

58⅞"

RAIL DETAIL (SIDE VIEW)

Rail

Thickness of siding or batten plus reveal

2×4 rail support

TOP AND BOTTOM PLATES

Stud location

90°

1. Miter bottom plates at 22½°, and mark stud position on both plates.

2. Cut and install jack studs, header, cripple studs, gussets, and rail.

FRAMING SUMMARY

Preassemble and erect the walls one at a time. You can cut all the studs to the same length, but cut each bottom plate to match its corresponding top plate to ensure square walls and plumb corners.

After you cut, preassemble, and erect three walls, check their fit. If they don't meet satisfactorily, you can build the remaining walls in place, measuring them to fit, instead of preassembling them.

The dimensions shown place the bottom of the header 80 inches above the floor, the height of a standard door. This allows you to install a door later. The walls accommodate either of the gusset designs on page 49 and the decorative bracket and panel designs on page 60.

ASSEMBLING THE WALLS

Use each top plate as a template to cut its corresponding bottom plate. Number the top and bottom plates. Mark the stud locations on the plates before assembling the frame,

INSTALLING WALL SECTIONS

1. Install first wall section with temporary bracing. Leave bracing in place until roof is installed.

2. Assemble, erect, plumb, and brace remaining walls.

3. Measure, cut, and install 1×12 facing.

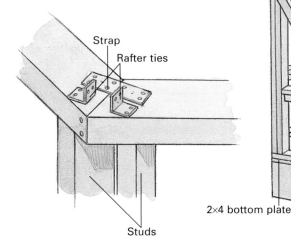

Strap

Rafter ties

Studs

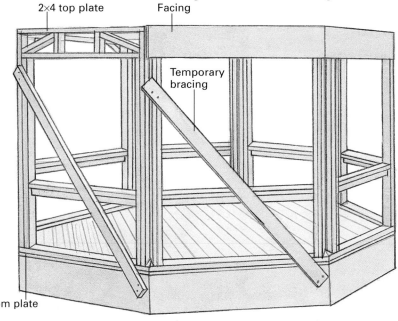

2×4 top plate

Facing

Temporary bracing

2×4 bottom plate

as illustrated on the opposite page, top left. Fasten the frame with 10d spiral nails. Face-nail the header through the posts.

The rail height above the floor varies, depending on your preference. Stand the first wall up and experiment with the height of the rail. When you find the height that looks pleasing to you, mark it on the studs. Nail the rail support 1½ inches below the mark, set back from the front of the studs by the thickness of the balusters you will install plus a ¼-inch reveal (see page 49). If the rail is a 2×4, assemble it as part of the wall frame. Rails 2×6 or wider are installed after the walls are up. (See "Notching a 2×6 Rail," below.) Fasten the support and rail to the studs with 10d finishing nails.

When the basic framing is completed, cut and install jack studs or trimmers to reduce the opening sizes, if you prefer.

ERECTING THE WALLS

Assembling walls is a one-person job, but putting up the walls is much easier with helpers. With a crew of two, one worker can hold the section in place while the other nails

it to the floor and adjoining wall.

Stand the first section on the floor, the outer edge of the bottom plate flush with the edge of the floor. Nail the bottom plate through the flooring with 10d spiral nails. Plumb the wall in both directions and brace it with 1×4s.

Put up the remaining walls the same way. Tie the top plate joints with metal straps as adjoining sections go up. Recheck the walls for plumb and attach perpendicular braces from the studs to the decking to keep the walls straight. Install diagonal bracing at least every other section. Leave the braces in place until you install the roof.

The 1×12 facing spans the studs, so wait until you have all the walls up before you nail it on. Determine the length of the facing boards by measuring the top plates from point to point on each facet. Cut the facing boards to that length with 22½-degree miter cuts at both ends. The interior and exterior boards are different lengths.

Install the facing boards to leave a ¼-inch reveal across the bottom of the header. If you want to build a shelf on the top plate, omit the interior facing. Drill holes for electrical wiring before installing the interior facing or trimming the corner studs.

NOTCHING A 2×6 RAIL

A 2×4 rail fits between the studs without any additional work. However, if you want to install a 2×6 rail because you like the way the extra width looks, you must notch it.

Start by cutting the rails about 1 foot longer than the distance between the studs. The extra length allows the boards to overlap so you can cut them to meet on the outside of the posts, as shown at right.

Cut notches at both ends, as shown. Put one rail in position (rail A). Lay the adjoining rail in place (rail B) with its tongue overlapping the one on rail A. To center a cutting line at the corner, mark the intersection on the front edge of the tongues, then use a square to carry the mark to the top of rail B. Stand a metal ruler on edge on the intersection point and push the other end into the V where the studs meet. Mark the line along the ruler. Cut rail B, then put it in place to draw the cutting line on rail A. Nail the outside miters when you install the rails.

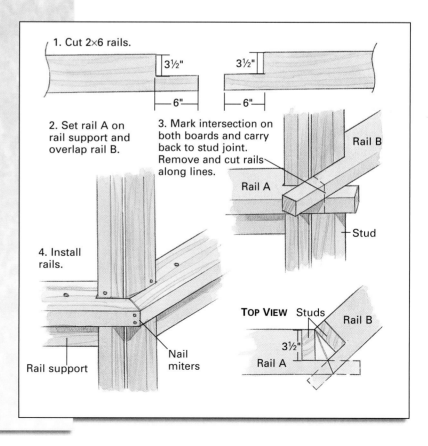

1. Cut 2×6 rails.

3½" 3½"

6" 6"

2. Set rail A on rail support and overlap rail B.

3. Mark intersection on both boards and carry back to stud joint. Remove and cut rails along lines.

Rail B

Rail A

Stud

4. Install rails.

Rail support

Nail miters

TOP VIEW Studs

Rail B

3½"

Rail A

INSTALLING THE ROOF

Because you have already fitted the rafters and sheathing, installing the roof is relatively easy. Have a helper or two when installing the rafters; do this in opposite pairs to keep the roof true.

RAISING THE RAFTERS

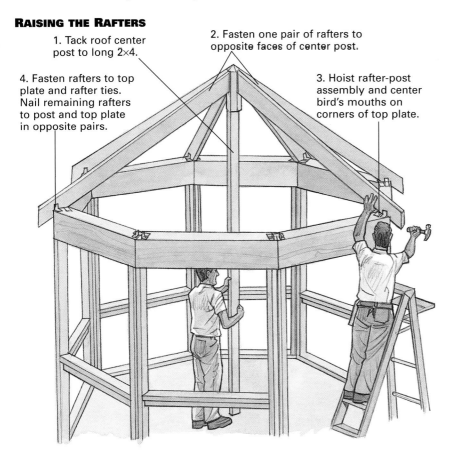

1. Tack roof center post to long 2×4.

2. Fasten one pair of rafters to opposite faces of center post.

4. Fasten rafters to top plate and rafter ties. Nail remaining rafters to post and top plate in opposite pairs.

3. Hoist rafter-post assembly and center bird's mouths on corners of top plate.

ROOFING THE GAZEBO

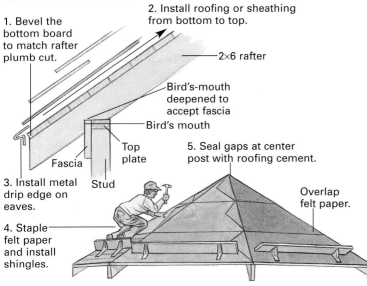

1. Bevel the bottom board to match rafter plumb cut.

2. Install roofing or sheathing from bottom to top.

2×6 rafter

Bird's-mouth deepened to accept fascia

Bird's mouth

Top plate

Fascia

Stud

3. Install metal drip edge on eaves.

4. Staple felt paper and install shingles.

5. Seal gaps at center post with roofing cement.

Overlap felt paper.

RAISING THE RAFTERS

To raise the roof, temporarily attach a long 2×4 to the bottom of the center post. Cut the top of the 2×4 square, and attach the center post with 2½-inch screws angled through opposite sides of the 2×4 into the bottom of the post. This way you can remove the 2×4 from below. Attach the first two rafters to opposite faces of the roof center post and tilt the assembly through the opening to rest on top of the walls.

Attach the rafters to the center post with construction adhesive and framing screws driven with a drill/driver. Support the rafter tails as you raise the assembly to keep the rafters from pulling away from the center post. Then set the rafters into the rafter ties and nail or screw them to the top plate. Fasten them into the rafter ties with framing-connector nails. Similarly attach the remaining rafters in opposing pairs. Remove the temporary 2×4.

ROOFING THE GAZEBO

You can install any roofing you prefer over the rafters. To install composition shingles over sheathing, bevel the bottom sheathing board or panel to the angle of the roof pitch, as shown in the bottom-left illustration. Use the table on page 88 to determine common pitch angles, or use a bevel gauge to match the roof angle.

Working from the bottom up, face-nail the sheathing to the rafters. You don't need to blind-nail them because the nails won't show. To keep the fasteners straight, lay the sheathing in place and snap chalk lines, centered on the rafters, on it. If you miss a rafter, remove and reposition the nail or screw.

Fasten metal drip edge along the eaves with nails of the same metal as the edging; dissimilar metals will corrode. Staple 15-pound roofing felt over the sheathing, starting at the bottom and overlapping each piece by 6 inches at the sides and bottom edges. Then nail on the shingles with ¾-inch roofing nails, which are short enough that their points won't show inside the gazebo. Cut shingles for the hips and install them from the roof edge to the center post, as shown on page 92. Then seal the top shingles at the center post with roofing cement and remove the wall braces. (See pages 90–97 for information on shingles.)

FINISHING AND TRIMMING

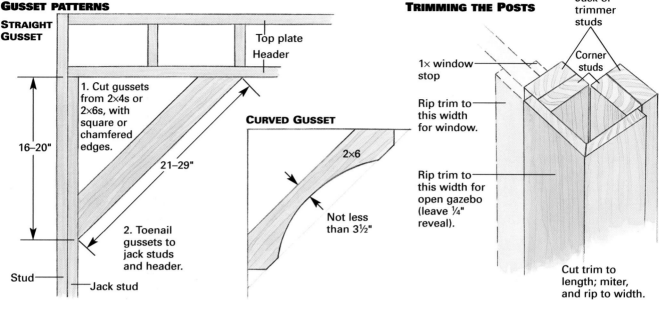

GUSSET PATTERNS

STRAIGHT GUSSET

Top plate
Header

1. Cut gussets from 2×4s or 2×6s, with square or chamfered edges.

16–20"

21–29"

2. Toenail gussets to jack studs and header.

Stud

Jack stud

CURVED GUSSET

2×6

Not less than 3½"

TRIMMING THE POSTS

Jack or trimmer studs

Corner studs

1× window stop

Rip trim to this width for window.

Rip trim to this width for open gazebo (leave ¼" reveal).

Cut trim to length; miter, and rip to width.

Finish the gazebo by installing gussets, post trim, and balusters. Pages 58–61 show decorative options.

INSTALLING THE GUSSETS

Gussets fit across the top corners of the openings. Their length and shape are matters of preference. To find the size you like best, start with a 2×4 that's 29 inches long, miter-cut at 45 degrees on both ends. Recut the miter at one end until you find a length you like. Then toenail the gusset to the studs with 10d nails. For curved gussets, make one overlength and test it by trimming from each end equally. Use the final one as a pattern.

TRIMMING THE POSTS

Rip the trim for the corner posts from a 1×6. If you added jack studs to make narrower openings, you'll probably have to rip the trim from a wider board.

Measure the distance between the floor and the 1×12 facing (or from the bottom of the skirt if you want to carry the post line to the bottom) and cut the trim to length. Miter one edge at 22½ degrees and rip the other edge to the width needed. Install the trim with a ¼-inch reveal, as shown above right. Fasten one piece of trim to the studs with 10d finish nails, apply construction adhesive along

the mitered edge, and nail on the second piece. Snug the miters with 8d finish nails 6 inches apart from opposite sides.

INSTALLING BALUSTERS

Before you install the balusters, check local codes for spacing requirements. Cut the 2×2 balusters to fit between the rail and the bottom plate. Chamfer the ends. If you plan to inset them, fasten a 2×2 nailer across the bottom plate to provide a nailing surface. Experiment with three or four balusters to determine an interval that looks pleasing to you within the range required by code.

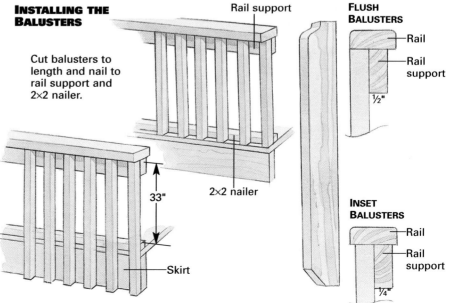

INSTALLING THE BALUSTERS

Rail support

Cut balusters to length and nail to rail support and 2×2 nailer.

33"

2×2 nailer

Skirt

FLUSH BALUSTERS

Rail

Rail support

½"

INSET BALUSTERS

Rail

Rail support

¼"

BUILDING AND INSTALLING A CUPOLA

A cupola is built like a small roof, then installed on top of the main roof. Originally cupolas were built with open sides and served as a vent, allowing hot air to rise up and escape the building so cooler air could flow into the structure.

Although some cupolas are made for ventilation, most now are purely decorative.

This cupola can be added to any gazebo and modified to suit the style of the structure. The gazebo shown here is the open gazebo illustrated on the previous pages.

When constructing a gazebo with a cupola, build the main roof first and staple felt paper onto it. Next install the cupola, and finally shingle both roofs at the same time.

DESIGN NOTES

The first question to ask when planning a cupola is: How high and wide should it be? The answer is a matter of style, so let your taste decide. Make scaled side-view drawings of the gazebo, and sketch different-size cupolas on top to get an idea of how each would look. Rafter length can vary according to diameter and height, but a cupola roof looks best when its pitch is the same as that of the main roof.

The cupola base sections are cut from 2×12s, which are tall enough to accommodate the rafters on even a steep 12/12 roof pitch. The length shown produces a cupola that's about 30 inches in diameter. For a different size, multiply the desired cupola diameter times .416 to determine the length of the facets.

The proportions of a 2×12 base suit gazebos that are between 8 and 12 feet in diameter and roof pitches that are from 6/12 to 12/12. A 2×8 base made with 10-inch sections fits a smaller gazebo. On a larger gazebo, make the cupola 3 to 4 feet in diameter with 2×6 cupola rafters.

To test your design, cut the pieces and assemble them with screws. Set the assembly on the main roof. If it looks too large or small, adjust the size of the base sections and recut the rafters. If the cupola looks too tall, for example, disassemble the base and rip the 2×12s to make them narrower.

OPEN GAZEBO WITH CUPOLA (PERSPECTIVE VIEW)

Octagonal center post

Beveled 2×4

Composition or other shingles

Felt paper

1× or plywood sheathing

2×4 rafter

2×12 collar

Collar tie

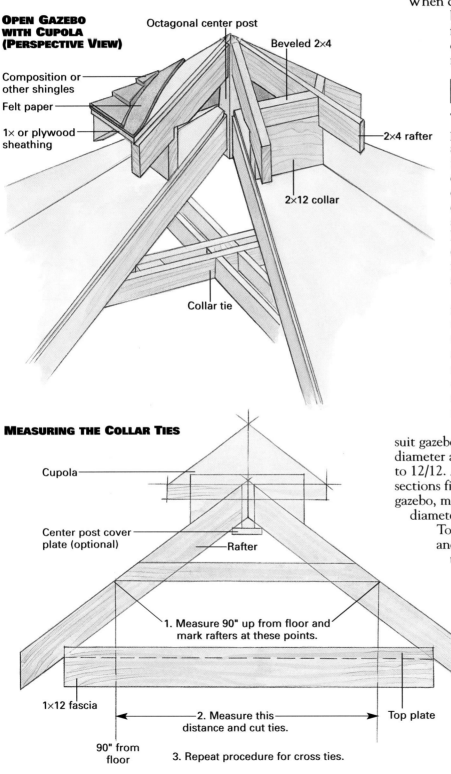

MEASURING THE COLLAR TIES

Cupola

Center post cover plate (optional)

Rafter

1. Measure 90" up from floor and mark rafters at these points.

1×12 fascia

2. Measure this distance and cut ties.

Top plate

90" from floor

3. Repeat procedure for cross ties.

MATERIALS LIST

MAIN STRUCTURE:
Same as open gazebo (pg. 41)
CUPOLA: (30-inch diameter)
Base	2×12×10', 2
Collar	2×4×8', 2
Post	4×4×3'
Rafters	2×4×10', 2
¾" sheathing	4×8, 1
Fascia	1×6×8', 2
Shingles	½ square

1. Toenail collar tie A to rafters.

2. Toenail board B to rafter and face-nail to board A.

3. Attach board C.

4. Face-nail spacer D to A.

5. Attach board E to rafters and spacer.

6. Toenail board F to E and to rafters.

7. Toenail board G to E and to rafters.

ASSEMBLING THE COLLAR TIES

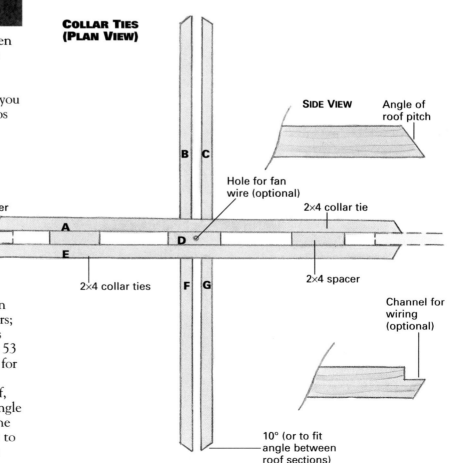

INSTALLING THE COLLAR TIES

Collar ties—boards attached between two rafters—keep the weight of the roof from pushing out on the walls. A 12-foot open gazebo without a cupola doesn't need collar ties, but you should install them on larger gazebos or any gazebo with a cupola. Make collar ties from 2×4 lumber for structures with 2×6 rafters; use 2×6s with 2×8 rafters. Install the collar ties before you put on the roofing or cupola.

Place collar ties 90 inches above the floor to accommodate the installation of a ceiling fan in an enclosed or screened gazebo. Make sure the span of the fan blades will clear the rafters; buy the fan or get the specifications before you install the ties. See page 53 for instructions on installing wiring for a ceiling fan.

The collar ties fit against the roof, so miter the top ends at the same angle as the roof. A 10-degree miter on the corners lets the collar ties fit snugly to the roof section. Don't install them square cut.

COLLAR TIES (PLAN VIEW)

SIDE VIEW   Angle of roof pitch

Hole for fan wire (optional)

2×4 collar tie

Rafter

2×4 collar ties

2×4 spacer

Channel for wiring (optional)

10° (or to fit angle between roof sections)

BUILDING AND INSTALLING A CUPOLA
continued

TESTING THE CUPOLA

FRONT View

Rafter length
(See chart below)

12–18"

2×4

Pitch	6/12	8/12	12/12
Rafter length	16½"	17⅞"	21¾"

Front View

2×4 collar

Side View

2×12 base

12½"

Bevel to match pitch of main roof.

1. Cut base sections to length, miter, and fasten at corners.

2. Cut cupola center post and rafters. Test rafter fit but do not fasten.

3. Cut collar sections, and miter but don't attach.

4. Cut sheathing and set aside.

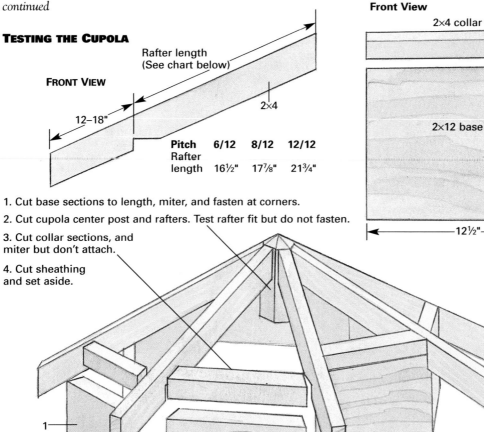

1

INSTALLING THE CUPOLA

1. Center base assembly on roof, toenail to roof decking, and install flashing.

Base assembly

Metal flashing

Collar

Rafter

Main roof with sheathing and felt paper installed

2. Attach rafters and collar to cupola base.

3. Install cupola sheathing, and shingle both roofs.

Cut the pieces in the order shown above. Cut the collar sections after you have fitted the rafters.

Assemble the base first. Miter the corners and bevel the bottom to match the pitch of the roof. Run a bead of construction adhesive on the mitered corners, and assemble the base with 8d finish nails. Test the rafters following the same procedures you used with the main roof. Cut the cupola sheathing and number all the pieces. Then install the base assembly on the main roof.

Center the cupola base on the main roof and toenail it to the main-roof rafters with 10d spiral nails. Install metal roof flashing around the bottom of the base, overlapping it at the corners. Then toenail the rafters to the base, and the collar sections to both the rafters and the base. Nail the sheathing sections onto the cupola rafters and install the felt paper. Then shingle both roofs.

STEPS AND WIRING

Constructing a step entrance to your gazebo or installing wiring for a ceiling fan or lighting are enhancements that you should incorporate into your design during the planning stages. Although you can add a step after you have completed the structure, it is easier to run wiring during construction.

BUILDING A STEP

Local codes specify floor heights that require a step at the entrance to your gazebo. Generally if the height from the ground to the floor is no more than 7 inches, a step isn't required. If your structure has a door in the entrance, however, most codes will require a runway. The runway allows you to open the door without having to back down the step and helps prevent falls when exiting the structure. Check with your local building department for requirements.

The runway is essentially a small floor attached to the main floor frame. Although you can attach it to the skirt or subskirt after completing the framing, it's best to measure, set, and cut the runway posts when laying out the structure. That way you can level and cut them to the same height as the others.

Use 2× stock for all framing members. Rip the lumber to conform to the height of your floor and local codes. Toenail the end joists and header to the top of the posts. Fasten the joists at the skirt with joist hangers, and trim the three exposed sides.

INSTALLING WIRING

The illustration at right shows one of several ways you can provide power to a ceiling fan or lights. Local building codes may require alternate methods. Codes also specify approved ways to run power from your main circuit panel to the gazebo. Make sure the fan blades will be at least 7 feet above the floor when the fan is installed.

Run the wiring after you've finished the framing, drilling holes for sheathed cable (14/2w/ground). Staple the cable about every 8 inches and cover it with a dadoed 2×2 raceway, if you want to hide it. Cut the cover plate from a 2×8 to fit the junction of the rafters at the height of the ceiling fan.

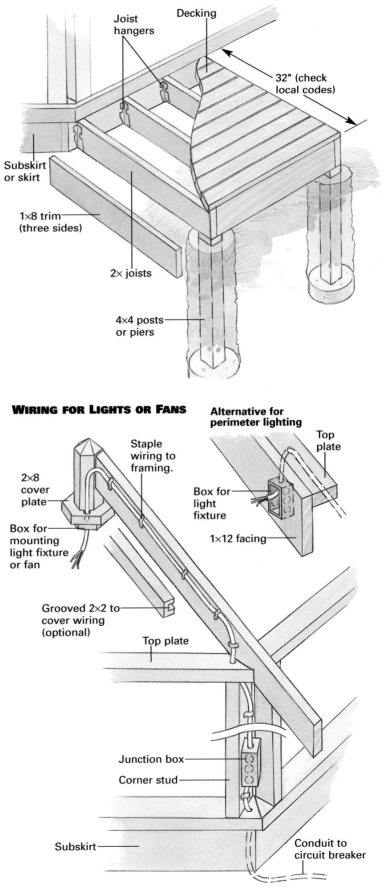

BUILDING A STEP

Joist hangers · Decking · 32" (check local codes) · Subskirt or skirt · 1×8 trim (three sides) · 2× joists · 4×4 posts or piers

WIRING FOR LIGHTS OR FANS · **Alternative for perimeter lighting**

2×8 cover plate · Staple wiring to framing. · Box for mounting light fixture or fan · Grooved 2×2 to cover wiring (optional) · Top plate · Top plate · Box for light fixture · 1×12 facing · Junction box · Corner stud · Subskirt · Conduit to circuit breaker

BUILDING A SCREENED GAZEBO

SCREENED GAZEBO

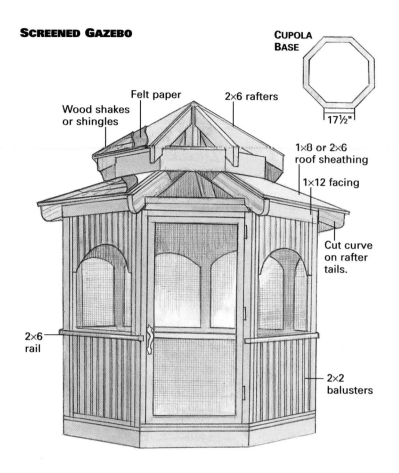

- Felt paper
- Wood shakes or shingles
- 2×6 rafters

CUPOLA BASE

17½"

- 1×8 or 2×6 roof sheathing
- 1×12 facing
- Cut curve on rafter tails.
- 2×6 rail
- 2×2 balusters

Framing for the 9-foot-diameter screened gazebo is similar to the larger open gazebo described on the previous pages. Modifications include provisions for the screen panels and the door, shown in the illustrations on these pages. You can modify this design to build a larger gazebo, but screen panels for openings wider than about 48 inches require center supports.

FRAMING NOTES

Lay out the site with the frame shown on page 40, measuring 9 feet from side to side. Each facet will be about 43½ inches long; place the diagonals 32¼ inches from the corners. Build the floor, walls, and main roof following the procedures on pages 42–48. Construct the cupola as shown on pages 50–52. Build both roofs with an 8/12 pitch. The rafter length for the main roof (measured from peak to outer plate edge) is 70⅞ inches; for the cupola roof, 25¼ inches.

■ **INSTALLING THE DOOR:** To install a door, add jack studs to the entry opening to create a rough opening. Use either of the methods shown on the opposite page. For a door that is hinged to the framing, make a rough opening as wide as the door plus ¼ inch. To hang the door in a jamb, buy or build the jamb first, then make a rough opening to fit it. Position the jack studs to center the rough opening in the wall. The

INSTALLING SCREEN PANELS

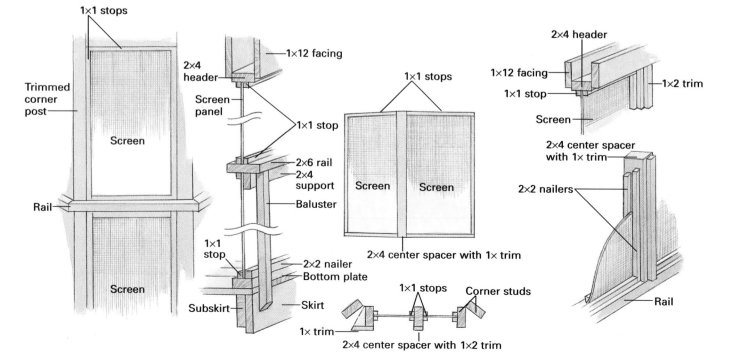

- 1×1 stops
- Trimmed corner post
- Screen
- Rail
- Screen
- Subskirt
- 1×1 stop
- 2×2 nailer
- Bottom plate
- Skirt
- 1× trim
- 1×12 facing
- 2×4 header
- Screen panel
- 1×1 stop
- 2×6 rail
- 2×4 support
- Baluster
- 1×1 stops
- Screen
- Screen
- 2×4 center spacer with 1× trim
- 1×1 stops
- Corner studs
- 2×4 center spacer with 1×2 trim
- 2×4 header
- 1×12 facing
- 1×1 stop
- 1×2 trim
- Screen
- 2×4 center spacer with 1× trim
- 2×2 nailers
- Rail

door shown is a commercial screen door with batters added to match the design.

■ **INSTALLING THE RAILS:** Install notched 2×6 rails, as shown on page 47. Attach the rail support flush with the front edge of the studs so the balusters can extend down over the skirting.

■ **INSTALLING BATTENS AND BALUSTERS:** Cut the 2×2 balusters and window battens. Chamfer the edges, and nail the battens 3 inches on center to the rail support and skirting. Tack the window battens to the fascias above the openings. Make a cardboard template of the curve and trace the curve onto the battens. Remove the battens, cut them, and nail them on.

FRAMING THE DOOR

FRAMING A WIDE OPENING

1. Measure opening between corner studs. Subtract width of door + ¼".

FRAMING A NARROW OPENING

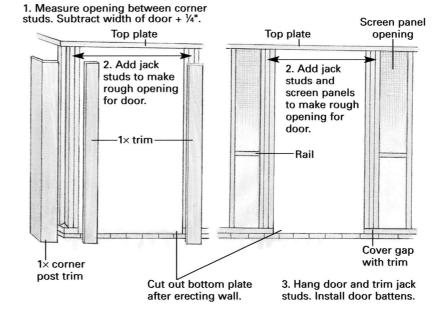

- Top plate
- 2. Add jack studs to make rough opening for door.
- 1× trim
- 1× corner post trim
- Cut out bottom plate after erecting wall.
- Top plate
- Screen panel opening
- 2. Add jack studs and screen panels to make rough opening for door.
- Rail
- Cover gap with trim
- 3. Hang door and trim jack studs. Install door battens.

■ **INSTALLING THE SCREENS:** Cut two sets of 1×1 stops to fit each opening. Nail in the outer stops. Measure each opening and make a screen panel for it with standard fiberglass screening and metal frame members available from home centers or lumberyards. Install the screens and nail in the inner stops to hold them.

MATERIALS LIST

FOUNDATION, FLOOR, AND WALLS
Posts	4×4×10', 4
Joists	2×6×10', 8
Subskirt	2×6×10', 4
Skirt	2×8×10', 4
Deck	2×6×8', 6
	2×6×10', 13
Studs, plates	2×4×8', 48
Header trim	1×12×8', 8
Sill	2×6×10', 4
Rail support	2×4×10', 4
Balusters and battens	2×2×8', 60

ROOF
Area	160 sq. ft.
Shingles	2 squares
Rafters	2×6×10', 8
Fascia	1×8×10', 4
Roof boards	1×8×10', 26
or tongue-and-groove	2×6×10, 40
■ OSB or plywood	4×8, 7
Trim	1×8×12', 12

CUPOLA (42-INCH DIAMETER)
Base	2×12×14', 2
■ Collar	2×4×12', 2
Rafters	2×4×12', 2
¾" sheathing	4×8, 1
■ Fascia	1×6×10', 2
Shingles	½ square

CUTTING WINDOW BATTENS

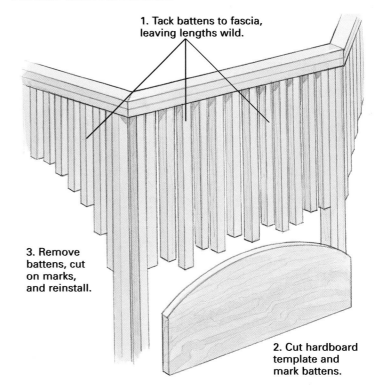

1. Tack battens to fascia, leaving lengths wild.
2. Cut hardboard template and mark battens.
3. Remove battens, cut on marks, and reinstall.

BUILDING AN ENCLOSED GAZEBO

ENCLOSED GAZEBO (PERSPECTIVE VIEW)

CUPOLA BASE

Rafter length (see chart)

15½"

Pitch	6/12	8/12	12/12
Rafter length	20⅞"	22⅝"	26⅞"

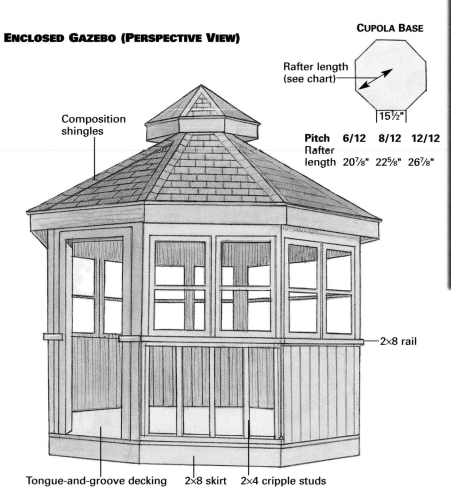

Composition shingles

2×8 rail

Tongue-and-groove decking   2×8 skirt   2×4 cripple studs

An enclosed gazebo offers multiseasonal enjoyment. This one is the same size as the open gazebo shown on pages 40–48 and is built the same way. Cripple studs are added to each lower wall section to facilitate siding, as shown in the illustration on the opposite page, and 2×8 blocking closes the openings between the rafters.

The windows are vinyl replacement windows, available at home centers and lumberyards. These units are designed to fit into existing openings and can be made to any size at reasonable cost. Many home centers stock the windows in standard sizes; simply adjust your rough openings to fit them.

FRAMING NOTES

A variety of siding choices give the enclosed gazebo a wide range of design possibilities. The one shown has 1×6 tongue-and-groove vertical siding inside and outside. Clapboard, shiplap, and other horizontal siding work just as well.

MATERIALS LIST

FRAMING:
Same materials used for 12-foot open gazebo (page 41)

ADDITIONAL MATERIAL:
- Mullions   2×4×10', 4
- Trim   1×3×8', 6
- Stops   1×1×8', 38
- Framing   2×4×10', 10
- Siding   170 sq. ft.
- Interior wainscoting
  1×8×8', 24
- Exterior base   1×8, 48'
- Interior baseboard   40'
- Door and hardware
- Vinyl or vinyl-clad windows (or other material of choice)

■ **FRAMING THE FLOOR:** Follow the layout and framing techniques shown for the open gazebo (see pages 40–49), except for the skirt. For this gazebo the exterior siding attaches to the subskirt and extends all the way to the bottom.

■ **FRAMING THE WALLS:** Buy the windows (or get accurate dimensions for them) before you build the walls. Build each wall section as a preassembled unit as illustrated, opposite, adding cripple studs in the bottom opening and spacing them 16 inches on center. Be sure to include the center 2×4 window support in your framing. If you use windows whose combined width doesn't fill the frame, reduce the opening with additional jack studs as you would the entrance opening. Construct the entrance wall as shown on page 55 for the screened gazebo, reducing the opening to the size of the rough door opening. Note that this design uses a horizontal 2×4 rail support; determine your rail height and toenail the support to the studs 1½ inches below it. Then install the lower cripple studs.

■ **INSTALLING THE RAIL:** The additional thickness of interior and exterior siding requires a 7-inch rail to provide an appropriate overhang. Notching this rail is slightly more complicated than cutting a 2×6 rail, so you may want to cut a couple of trial patterns before working on the finished stock. Snug the ends of the miters with construction adhesive and 8d finish nails.

■ **FRAMING THE ROOF:** The only difference between the roof framing on an

FRAMING THE WALLS

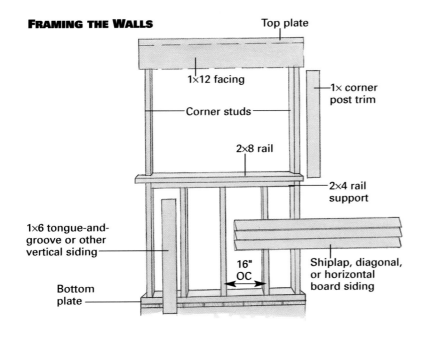

Top plate

1×12 facing

Corner studs

1× corner post trim

2×8 rail

2×4 rail support

1×6 tongue-and-groove or other vertical siding

16" OC

Shiplap, diagonal, or horizontal board siding

Bottom plate

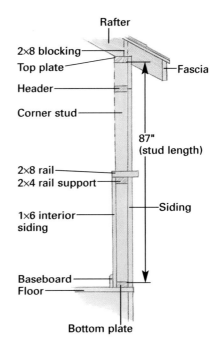

Rafter

2×8 blocking

Top plate

Fascia

Header

Corner stud

87" (stud length)

2×8 rail
2×4 rail support

1×6 interior siding

Siding

Baseboard
Floor

Bottom plate

enclosed gazebo and other structures is that you must fill the open spaces between rafters. Build the walls first, then install the rafters using the techniques discussed on pages 44–45 and 48. Measure the distance between each of the rafters and cut 2×8 blocking to fit. Miter the top of the blocking at the same angle as the roof pitch, and toenail the blocking to the top plate and the rafters.

■ **FRAMING THE WINDOWS:** Measure the opening, top to bottom and side to side, to order the windows. The 1× stops on the interior and 1× trim on the exterior retain the windows. Install the stops first, then set the window unit in the opening and fasten the trim. Caulk around the window frame.

ROOF DETAIL

1. Install rafters.

2. Cut 2×8 blocking and toenail between rafters.

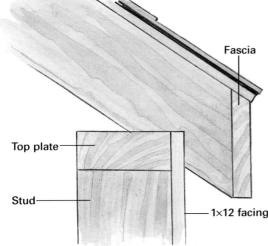

Fascia

Top plate

Stud

1×12 facing

MAKING THE RAILING

1. Rip 2×8 to 7" and cut it 14" longer than rough opening.

2. Cut four rails to pattern 1 and four rails to pattern 2.

3. Set pattern 1 loosely in opening and place pattern 2 on top. Scribe a line, and cut pattern 1 at corners. Repeat for doorway rails.

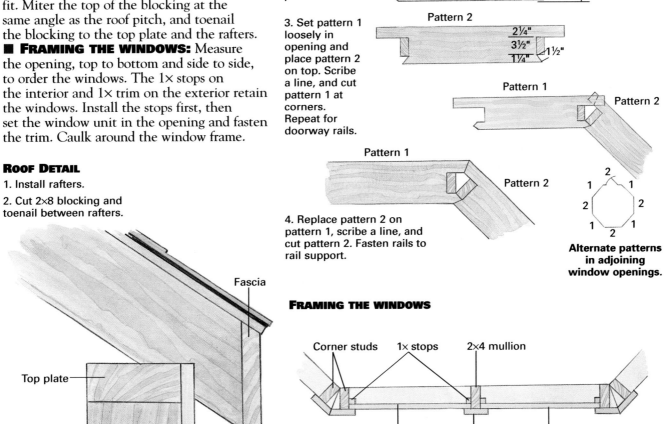

Pattern 1

7"

2¼"
3½"
1½"

1½"

7"

Pattern 2

2¼"
3½"
1¼"

1½"

Pattern 1

Pattern 2

Pattern 1

Pattern 2

2
1   1
2   2
1   1
2

Alternate patterns in adjoining window openings.

4. Replace pattern 2 on pattern 1, scribe a line, and cut pattern 2. Fasten rails to rail support.

FRAMING THE WINDOWS

Corner studs   1× stops   2×4 mullion

Window   1× trim   Window

DECORATIVE DETAILS

SPINDLE PATTERNS

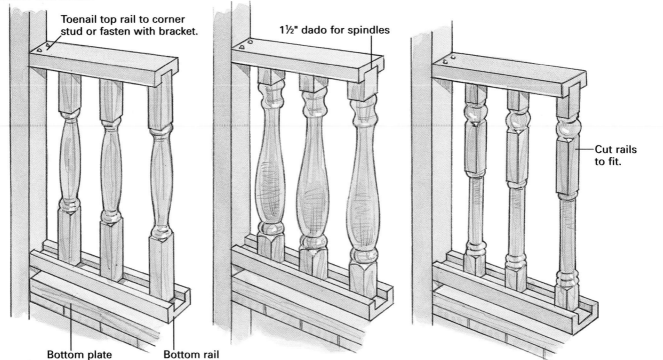

Toenail top rail to corner stud or fasten with bracket.

1½" dado for spindles

Cut rails to fit.

Bottom plate

Bottom rail

Customize your gazebo to match your home or landscape style by adorning it with spindle railings, slat railings, corner brackets, or friezes. You can add these elements to any gazebo.

READY-MADE OR DIY?

You can purchase many design components from lumberyards or home centers, or you can make your own if you have a moderately well-equipped home workshop. A local millwork shop usually offers custom parts and may have some stock items too, but expect to pay a substantially higher price there than at a home center.

■ **INSPECT THE STOCK:** Ready-made spindles and other decorative elements are usually made from treated stock or naturally resistant species such as redwood and cedar. No matter what the wood, inspect the product carefully. Avoid any parts that are cracked or warped. Commercial turnings are sometimes rough and require sanding before painting. Preassembled rail sections are often fastened with staples—make sure the joints are tight.

LET THEM WEEP

Rainwater that collects in the dadoes on the bottom rails may eventually rot balusters and slats and damage the rails. To let the moisture drain out of the dadoes, drill ³⁄₁₆-inch holes in the bottom of the groove before you assemble the railing. Space the holes about 6 inches apart.

RAILINGS, BALUSTERS, AND SPINDLES

Turned spindles cost only slightly more than square-cut 2×2s and are almost as strong as uncut stock.

Whether you purchase a commercial rail or make your own, you first need to decide the rail height. Measure the length of the railing between the posts and calculate the height of the spindles, slats, or other insert. The method you use to mount the railing inserts affects the length needed. You can mount the bottom of balusters, spindles, slats, or lattice either in a grooved rail (like the top rail) or between stops or nailers, as shown on page 49. Choose the method most appropriate to your skills, tools, and the look you want to achieve. If you're shopping for ready-made units, take the measurements with you.

To make spindle rails, cut each rail section to length and form a 1½-inch groove about ¾ inch deep along the center of each rail. Cut the groove with a table saw. Lay out the spindles on a flat surface to experiment with the spacing—about 3¾ inches between spindles works for most designs.

Clamp each pair of rails together, ends flush, and mark the center and edges of the spindles on both rails. Start 8d finishing nails into each rail at the marks, and assemble the sections. Drive the nails into the spindles until they just pierce the bottom of the groove. To avoid nailheads showing on the top rail, clamp the assembly in bar clamps and toenail each spindle to the top rail with two 6d finishing nails driven from underneath the top rail.

If your marks are accurate, the installed spindles will be plumb. To be doubly sure, nail the spindles in the bottom rail only, fasten both top and bottom rails with the spindles loose in the top dado, and as you face-nail or toenail each spindle at the top rail, use a 2-foot level to keep it plumb. Set the nails with a nail set, if necessary, fill, and sand smooth.

CUTTING DECORATIVE SLATS

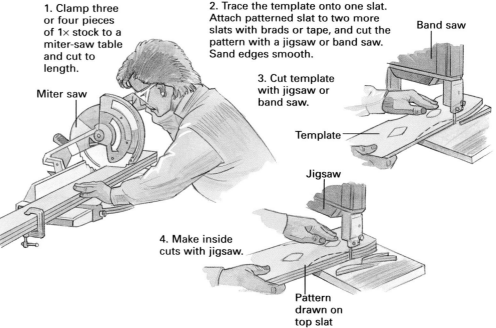

1. Clamp three or four pieces of 1× stock to a miter-saw table and cut to length.

Miter saw

2. Trace the template onto one slat. Attach patterned slat to two more slats with brads or tape, and cut the pattern with a jigsaw or band saw. Sand edges smooth.

Band saw

3. Cut template with jigsaw or band saw.

Template

Jigsaw

4. Make inside cuts with jigsaw.

Pattern drawn on top slat

SLAT RAILINGS

Slat railings offer many design possibilities. You can use one of the patterns illustrated below, or you can create your own. Start by dividing the distance between the studs by the width of an untrimmed 1×3, 1×4, or 1×6—whichever fits the opening most evenly and is wide enough for the pattern. Trim all the slats to a width that fits the opening when spaced at $\frac{3}{8}$ to $\frac{1}{2}$ inch apart and at each end, then tailor the pattern to this width.

To enlarge a pattern, glue graph paper with a $\frac{1}{4}$-inch grid to a piece of hardboard the same length as the slat. Duplicate the pattern on the hardboard, and use a jigsaw or scroll saw to cut out the template. Then clamp the template to two or three slats, and trace the outline on the top board. Remove the template and cut the slats. Don't cut the slats with the template still attached; repeated cutting against the template could change its shape or damage it. Fasten the slats to the rails in $\frac{3}{4}$-inch dadoes or between 1× nailers.

SLAT PATTERNS

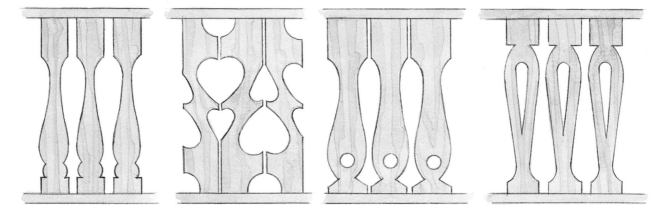

1× slats require a $\frac{3}{4}$" dado or nailers spaced $\frac{3}{4}$" apart

DECORATIVE DETAILS
continued

INSTALLING LATTICE

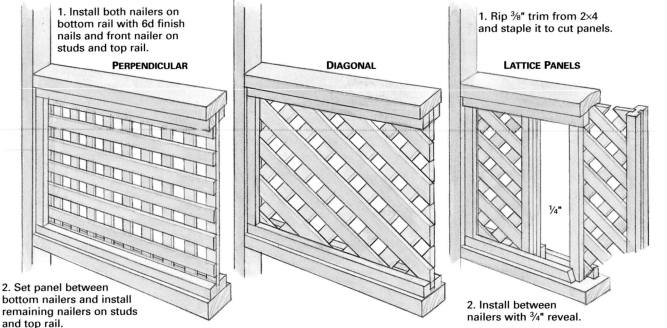

1. Install both nailers on bottom rail with 6d finish nails and front nailer on studs and top rail.

PERPENDICULAR

DIAGONAL

LATTICE PANELS

1. Rip ⅜" trim from 2×4 and staple it to cut panels.

¼"

2. Set panel between bottom nailers and install remaining nailers on studs and top rail.

2. Install between nailers with ¾" reveal.

DECORATIVE CORNER BRACKETS

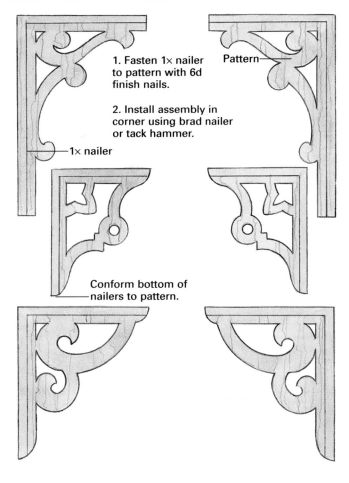

1. Fasten 1× nailer to pattern with 6d finish nails.

Pattern

2. Install assembly in corner using brad nailer or tack hammer.

1× nailer

Conform bottom of nailers to pattern.

INSTALLING LATTICE PANELS

Used as railing inserts and friezes, lattice panels cost less than traditional rail inserts.

Lumberyards and home centers sell lattice panels made of redwood, cedar, pressure-treated lumber, and plastic in several thicknesses. Using plastic panels in a painted wood gazebo is not advisable, however. No matter how high the quality of the plastic, the difference between plastic lattice and the surrounding wood structure is always noticeable. Choose ⅜-inch lattice for your railings and friezes; it resists warping and splitting better than thinner stock.

CORNER BRACKETS

Gingerbread, bric-a-brac, and carpenter's lace are names often applied to the fancy design elements of the Victorian period. Many home centers and lumberyards carry a wide array of decorative elements, including spindles, friezes, and corner brackets. Because making them is labor-intensive, however, they are expensive. You can make your own with a scroll saw.

Start with straight-grain, knot-free 1× or 2× stock, depending on how you will use the brackets in your gazebo. Use 2× stock for brackets that are attached to 2× framing members, 1× stock where they mate with

DECORATIVE FRIEZES

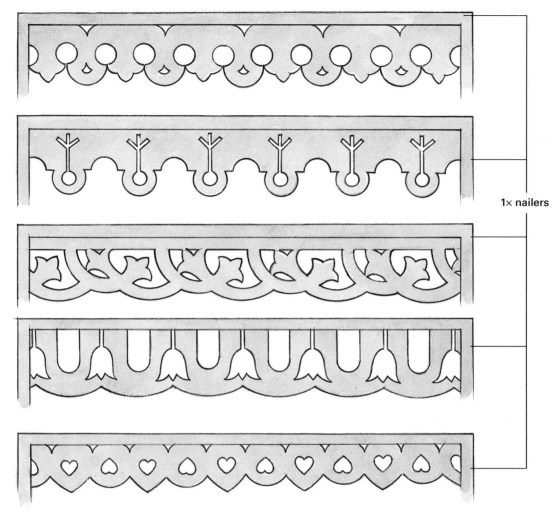

1× nailers

trim boards. Lay out the longest dimension of the pattern along the grain. Make a template as described on page 59 for making slats, and cut the corner brackets. Note that the edges are ¾ inch wider than they appear in the illustration. This edge will be hidden by the nailer.

Measure the nailer to the length of the bracket, miter the corners, and conform the bottom end to the design. Assemble the bracket and nailers and attach this assembly in the corner with brads. You won't have room to swing a full-size hammer in this task—toenail the nailers to the studs and header with a brad nailer or drive 6d finish nails straight in with a tack hammer.

FRIEZES

A frieze is a decorative band that spans the openings in your gazebo, much as a valance spans a window in your kitchen. Gazebo friezes, however, tend to be a lot more ornate than valances.

Use one piece of clear, straight 1× stock long enough to span each opening. Use the same methods for creating a template as you would for a slat rail pattern, transferring the pattern to hardboard and cutting the frieze. Note that if your pattern repeats itself within the span, you needn't cut it to the full width. Just lift it, reposition it, and continue tracing. To ensure the pattern finishes evenly at both ends, start it in the center of the frieze. Assemble the frieze to the nailers with 6d finishing nails, and fasten the nailers to the headers with 6d nails. Use a brad nailer or tack hammer.

FINISH FIRST

If you're applying finish to your railing, stain, seal, or paint the inserts and any dadoes before assembling the railing. You'll save time and achieve more complete coverage, and protection, of all surfaces.

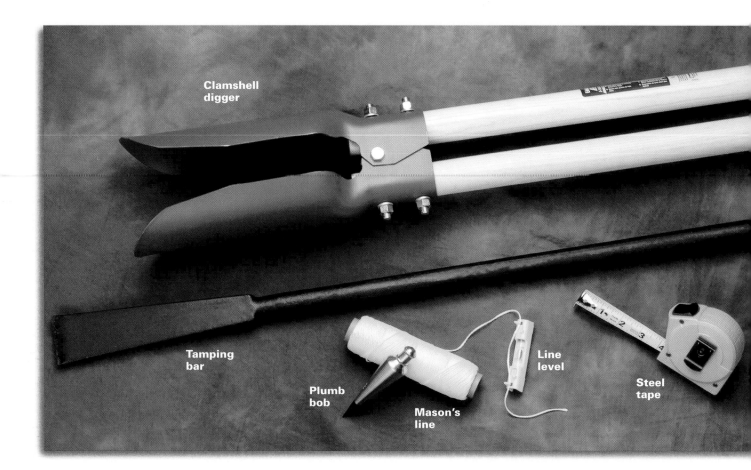

Clamshell digger

Tamping bar

Plumb bob

Mason's line

Line level

Steel tape

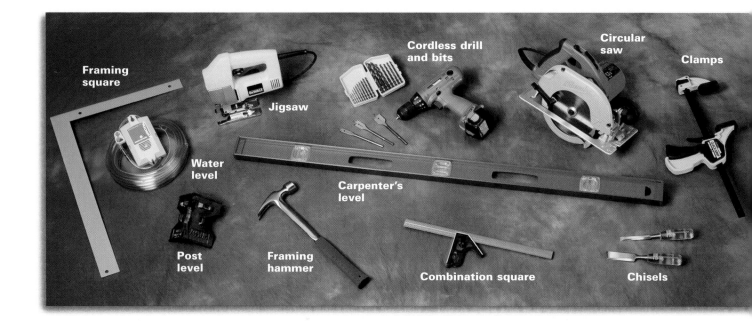

Framing square

Jigsaw

Cordless drill and bits

Circular saw

Clamps

Water level

Carpenter's level

Post level

Framing hammer

Combination square

Chisels

BUILDING BASICS

Whether you're building a shed or a gazebo, many of the same basic construction techniques and practices apply. In this chapter you'll find everything you need to know to build the structures illustrated in this book. Even if you consider yourself an old hand at building, you'll find a tip or two that makes the job go more smoothly. Information and advice on everything from buying lumber to methods for installing roofing and siding can be found. Use this chapter as a reference for the projects in this book and other projects.

Before you begin construction, inventory both your tools and your skills. Follow the guidelines below if you need to buy tools. If you run into an aspect of the work that's unfamiliar or that you're uncomfortable with, ask a contractor or a knowledgeable friend.

A contractor might charge you for time spent answering your questions, but the cost will save you time and money in the long run. In some cases, you may decide it's better to hire a professional to do a portion of the work. The information in this section can help you that decision.

Construction projects are noisy, hectic, and wearing. Minimize the effect of inevitable snags by organizing your work in a logical sequence and by allowing enough time to complete each portion. Wear a tool belt or use a bucket with a tool apron to keep your tools organized and out of the way. When you're done with a tool, return it to the same place every time so you won't waste time looking for it. Keep materials organized. Stack lumber to minimize warping and damage. Cover materials to protect them from weather. Keep the work site tidy, and make a separate pile for scrap wood.

SAFETY FIRST

Building a shed or gazebo can be great fun, as long as you make safety a top priority. You wouldn't want to mar an otherwise enjoyable experience with injuries.
■ Wear safety glasses or goggles when using power tools or striking tools. Get the kind of goggles that have side protectors.
■ Wear a dust mask when sawing.
■ Don't use power tools in the rain or in wet locations. Always unplug them before making adjustments, and make sure the switch is off before plugging them in.
■ Wear clothing that fits snugly. Loose sleeves or jewelry can get caught in power tools or even on the work.
■ Make sure ladders are supported on level surfaces before climbing them. Set them close enough to the work so you don't have to overreach. Don't set tools on a stepladder where you can't see them.
■ Use roof jacks when you are roofing.

RULES FOR TOOLS

If you have any experience with home maintenance or basic construction, you may already own many of the tools you need to build your shed or gazebo. If you need to add to your tool chest, consider these suggestions:
■ Buy the best tools you can afford. Cheap tools wear out quickly, can be dangerous, and cost more in the long run.
■ Add a 100-foot drop cord, rated for outdoor use, to your tool inventory.
■ Buy power tools with double insulation for safety. When you will use a tool frequently or for other projects—a circular saw or drill, for example—buy a heavy-duty model with better bearings and a more-powerful motor for greater durability.
■ Garage sales and flea markets might be good sources for bargain hand tools, but buy power tools new, and buy respected brands.
■ Rent the tools you will use infrequently. Ask the rental staff for instructions on safe and proper use. Have the work ready when you rent the tool, so you're not paying for the tool to be idle.

BUYING LUMBER

Pound for pound, wood is almost as strong as steel. Its warm, natural beauty and remarkable workability make it ideal for shed and gazebo construction. Not all woods are alike, however. Select wood for your project based on appearance, cost, and durability.

SPECIES

Several species resist decay and insects, making them ideal for outdoor structures. Here's a brief summary of their characteristics.

REDWOOD, CEDAR, AND CYPRESS: Unmatched for their beauty, these species are naturally resistant to weathering, warping, cupping, shrinkage, and insect damage, but they carry a higher price tag than other woods (redwood is the most costly). Untreated, they weather to a silvery gray, or if you prefer, you can easily color them with stain. Cedar tends to split easily, and cypress may be hard to find outside its natural growth areas.

Only the heartwood is naturally resistant to decay. Use heartwood for posts and structural members fastened near or close to the ground; use sapwood treated with a sealer for rails, studs, and boards that will be visible.

FIR AND PINE: These species are strong, lightweight, widely available, and less expensive than naturally resistant woods. They are available in two forms: untreated lumber and pressure-treated lumber.

UNTREATED LUMBER: This stock is susceptible to outdoor weathering and decay if left unfinished. Not suitable for posts at all, it can be used for nonstructural members if painted.

PRESSURE-TREATED LUMBER: A less-expensive substitute for redwood, cedar, and cypress, pine and fir that have been treated with chemicals under pressure are extremely rot-resistant.

Both chromated copper arsenate (CCA)—identifiable by its green tinge—and ammoniacal copper arsenate (ACA) have been used widely, but wood treated with these and other arsenic compounds will not be available for residential use after December 2003. Ammoniacal copper quaternary ammonia (ACQ), a newer preservative, will remain available. Grade stamps tell which chemical has been used. They also tell how much preservative the lumber holds. Posts and boards that contact, or are close to, the ground (skids, joists, and skirts) should have

SHEET GOODS

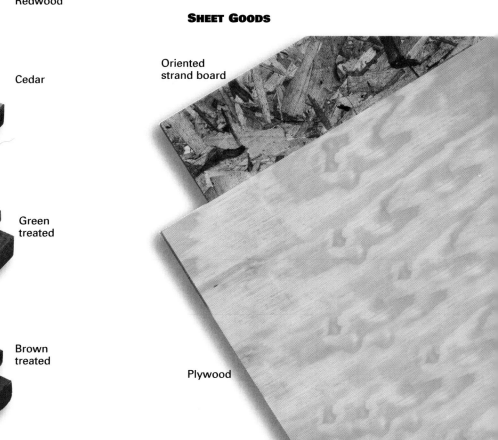

Redwood

Cedar

Green treated

Brown treated

Oriented strand board

Plywood

a retention level of 0.60 or higher. Lumber treated to 0.40 works sufficiently for other components. Look for a "Ground Contact" or "LP22" marking.

LUMBER GRADES

Lumber is divided into categories according to its thickness. *Boards* are less than 2 inches thick, and *dimension lumber* is 2 to 4 inches thick. Lumber is graded for its strength and appearance in accordance with standards established by independent agencies.

BOARDS: Fir and pine boards are graded in two categories: select and common.

SELECT: This is the best grade, with few or no knots or blemishes. Select grades are labeled A–D.

- **A:** contains no knots
- **B:** has only small blemishes
- **C:** has some minor defects
- **D:** has larger blemishes that can be concealed with paint

COMMON: Utility board grades are ranked from 1 to 5 in descending quality. A middle grade, such as number 3, is a good choice for most projects.

WORKING WITH PRESSURE-TREATED LUMBER

Pressure treatment is not a substitute for finishing the wood. A couple of weeks after construction, apply water-repellent sealer—several coats on surfaces you have cut.

After two to three months, apply paint or stain, and after that, refinish pressure-treated stock from time to time. Unfinished treated wood gradually turns to a weathered gray. Paint and other protective finishes help structures last longer.

Wear gloves when handling treated wood and a respirator when sawing it. Don't burn or bury the scrap. Check with your local environmental agency for proper disposal methods.

DIMENSION LUMBER: There are three grades of fir and pine dimension lumber.

- **CONSTRUCTION GRADE:** strongest, fewest defects
- **STANDARD GRADE:** almost as good as construction grade, but less expensive
- **UTILITY GRADE:** unsuitable for framing Pressure-treated lumber is also graded.

Buy at least standard-grade dimension lumber and common-grade number 3 boards for the projects in this book. Buy better grades where appearance is critical.

GRADE STAMPS: WHAT THEY MEAN

Manufacturers stamp their wood products to provide customers with information about the species, prevalence of defects, grade, and moisture content. A grade stamp may also carry a number or the name of the mill that produced it and a certification symbol that shows the lumber association whose grading standards are used.

Pressure-treated lumber carries a grade stamp that shows the year it was treated, the chemical used as a preservative, exposure condition (whether it can be used above ground or ground contact), and the amount of chemical treatment it received.

Plywood grade stamps also show whether the wood is suitable for ground contact or only for aboveground use and whether it can be used as sheathing. The stamp also specifies the thickness of the sheet and the distance it can span between rafters and joists. If the plywood is made to withstand exposure to the weather, such as siding for a shed, it is marked as exterior-grade.

Many projects fail because the lumber used wasn't suited to a specific application. Grade stamps help you choose lumber that meets your project's requirements.

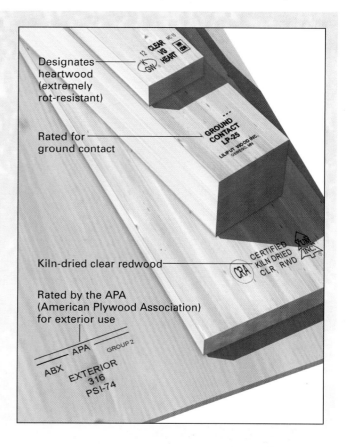

Designates heartwood (extremely rot-resistant)

Rated for ground contact

Kiln-dried clear redwood

Rated by the APA (American Plywood Association) for exterior use

BUYING LUMBER

continued

SEASONING

Most wood is either air dried or kiln dried. Marks specify the wood's moisture content: S-GRN (green lumber), over 19 percent moisture content; S-DRY, up to 19 percent; MC 15, up to 15 percent.

For framing and rough work, air-dried lumber is adequate, but S-DRY or MC 15 lumber is better. Dry stock warps less, works more easily, holds fasteners more tightly, and finishes better. Always use dry for finish work.

NOMINAL VERSUS ACTUAL

The dimensions that describe the size of lumber, such as 1×4, 2×4, or 2×6, are nominal, not actual, dimensions. They indicate the size of the stock when it was cut from the log, before drying and milling reduced its size. Actual dimensions of nominal lumber sizes are shown in "What Size Is It, Really?" on the opposite page.

Shrinkage is generally consistent from one kind of lumber to another, although pressure-treated boards may vary slightly from untreated boards. If exact size is significant to your design, measure the actual dimensions. For example, when planning a gazebo deck made of 1×6 decking, you'll want to know exactly how many boards will fit across the span of the floor, so measure the stock before fastening it.

PLYWOOD

Manufacturers produce plywood in a variety of sizes, thicknesses, textures, species, and grades. Plywood used for outdoor construction must be an exterior-grade material made with glue that does not deteriorate when exposed to moisture.

Purchase AA exterior grade for sheathing that you will stain or paint. Lesser grades work well for flooring, roof sheathing, or sheathing covered with siding, but they have blemishes that show through paint or stain. Grade stamps give you most of the information you need in buying plywood.

LOOK BEFORE BUYING

No lumber is perfect. To get good materials for your project, walk around the lumberyard. Take your project plans with you. Look at different species and grades to compare their colors, grain patterns, and quality. Compare pressure-treated with untreated products.

Ask a salesperson to recommend project materials. The retailer also can give you an idea of relative costs for various materials.

Shop around to compare both material costs and service. You might find a higher-grade stock costs less at one yard than lower

COMMON LUMBER FLAWS

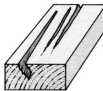
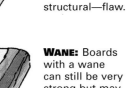

CHECKS: Splits that run perpendicular to the grain are called checks, a cosmetic—not a structural—flaw.

SHAKES: Splits following the grain will probably grow larger. Do not use boards with splits that extend halfway or more.

KNOTS: Use these rules when using boards with knots for joists and rafters. 1. Tight knots are OK in the top third of the board. 2. Missing knots are OK in the middle third. 3. No knots larger than an inch in the bottom third. Loose knots usually fall out in time.

WANE: Boards with a wane can still be very strong but may not provide enough nailing surface for sheathing joints.

CUP: Cupped wood is strong but unsightly. If the cup is severe, the board may crack when you fasten it.

TWIST: If you use a twisted board, one or more corners will stick out. Eliminate minor twists by installing blocking and strategic fastening.

BOW: Bowed lumber is usually not a problem unless very pronounced. Straighten bowed studs or joists with blocking.

CROWN: The high part in the middle of a board is the crown. Face all the crowns the same way on a wall frame. On joists or rafters, put the crown up. Avoid badly crowned lumber or cut it into shorter pieces.

grade materials at another. If you can't get the material to the site yourself, add delivery charges to the cost of your material.

As you shop for lumber, check each board for defects. Common lumber flaws are shown opposite. Sight down the length of the board on both the face and the edge. Perfect lumber is rare, so look for the straightest, flattest boards you can find. Check for knots— small or tight ones are acceptable, but avoid boards with large, loose ones. Look for checks and splits. If the wood hasn't been kiln dried, more checks and splits will develop as the lumber seasons.

ESTIMATING, ORDERING, AND STORING

You can get a quick idea of project cost from your lumberyard visits, but ordering material requires more detail. Make a materials list that designates how much of each size stock you need, the quantity of each size, and the species you want. Be ready to tell the dealer what kind of footings you'll be using and how you will finish the structure. You may be able to negotiate a better price for materials if you place the full order with one supplier.

When the materials arrive, protect them from direct sunlight and moisture. If the lumber has not been kiln dried, let it dry for several weeks. Stack boards flat and evenly weighted, inserting spacers (called stickers) between them. Store them under a cover or in the shade. Kiln-dried lumber is ready to use right away; protect it from direct sunlight before you begin construction.

WHAT SIZE IS IT, REALLY?

After it is cut, lumber is dried, planed, and smoothed, all of which reduces its thickness and width. The nominal size of a board (for example, 1×4) refers to the size before drying and planing; actual size means the size you actually get.

Nominal Size	Actual Size
1×2	$\frac{3}{4}$" × $1\frac{1}{2}$"
1×3	$\frac{3}{4}$" × $2\frac{1}{2}$"
1×4	$\frac{3}{4}$" × $3\frac{1}{2}$"
1×6	$\frac{3}{4}$" × $5\frac{1}{2}$"
1×8	$\frac{3}{4}$" × $7\frac{1}{4}$"
1×10	$\frac{3}{4}$" × $9\frac{1}{4}$"
1×12	$\frac{3}{4}$" × $11\frac{1}{4}$"
2×2	$1\frac{1}{2}$" × $1\frac{1}{2}$"
2×4	$1\frac{1}{2}$" × $3\frac{1}{2}$"
2×6	$1\frac{1}{2}$" × $5\frac{1}{2}$"
2×8	$1\frac{1}{2}$" × $7\frac{1}{4}$"
2×10	$1\frac{1}{2}$" × $9\frac{1}{4}$"
2×12	$1\frac{1}{2}$" × $11\frac{1}{4}$"
4×4	$3\frac{1}{2}$" × $3\frac{1}{2}$"

When figuring board feet, make your calculations using the nominal size.

To figure board feet, multiply the thickness of the piece in inches times the width of the piece in inches. Multiply that number times the length of the piece in feet, then divide by 12. (Or multiply times the length in inches, then divide by 144.) For instance, a 2×4 that's 8 feet long contains $5\frac{1}{3}$ board feet: 2×4=8, 8×8 (length in feet)=64, 64/12=$5\frac{1}{3}$.

OSB

Oriented strand board (OSB) is a sheet material of compressed wood strands arranged in layers at right angles to each other. The strands are bonded with phenol-formaldehyde adhesive. OSB's strength and ability to hold fasteners make it an ideal—and less costly—alternative to plywood for sheathing and underlayment.

HOW FAR CAN JOISTS SPAN?

This table shows the lengths (feet-inches) that various species safely can span when joists are set 16 inches on center.

SPECIES	GRADE	2×6	2×8	2×10
California Redwood	Const. Heart or Const. Common	7-3	10-9	13-6
Western Cedars	Sel. Struct.	8-10	11-8	14-11
	No. 1	8-7	11-1	13-6
	No. 2	8-4	11-0	13-6
Douglas Fir	Sel. Struct.	13-7	17-4	21-1
	No. 1	13-1	16-5	19-1
	No. 2	12-7	15-5	17-10
Southern Pine	Sel. Struct.	13-4	17-0	20-9
	No. 1	13-1	16-9	20-4
	No. 2	12-10	16-1	18-10

Spans shown are for 40-pound live load—the standard required for residential floors.

FASTENERS

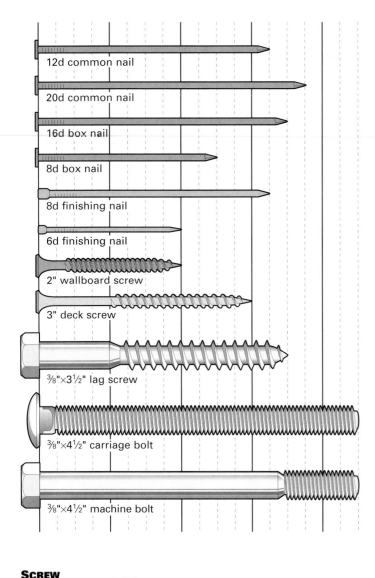

12d common nail

20d common nail

16d box nail

8d box nail

8d finishing nail

6d finishing nail

2" wallboard screw

3" deck screw

⅜"×3½" lag screw

⅜"×4½" carriage bolt

⅜"×4½" machine bolt

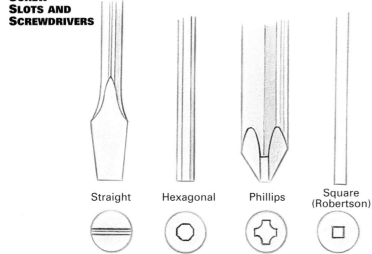

**SCREW
SLOTS AND
SCREWDRIVERS**

Straight   Hexagonal   Phillips   Square
(Robertson)

Don't scrimp on the quality or quantity of fasteners in your project. Construction fasteners come in a variety of forms—nails, screws, lag screws, bolts, and metal framing connectors. You may need one or more masonry fasteners, too, if you build your shed or gazebo on a slab or otherwise attach it to a concrete surface.

NAILS

Friction against the wood fibers holds nails in lumber. Nail sizes are expressed in pennies, abbreviated as *d*, as in 6d or 10d. The larger the number, the larger and longer the nail. Nails ordinarily used for projects include:

COMMON NAILS: Used for general construction, these have large heads and thick shanks. They hold well but may split the wood.

BOX NAILS: Thinner than common nails but the same length, box nails reduce splitting in ¾-inch or thinner stock. Cement-coated ones (CC box nails) hold best.

RINGSHANK AND SPIRAL-SHANKED NAILS: These grip wood fibers better than common or box nails and don't easily work their way out.

FINISHING NAILS: These have slender shanks and small heads that can be countersunk. Use them for trim work or wherever you don't want the heads to show.

CASING NAILS: These are heftier finishing nails that provide more holding power and often are used for exterior trim.

BRADS: These miniature finishing nails are used for attaching thin, fragile pieces.

DUPLEX NAILS: These double-head nails are handy for temporary bracing. When driven in, the second head makes them easy to pull out.

Rust-resistant nails are best for outdoor projects. Most types of nails are available galvanized, and some are available made of other rust-resistant metals.

GALVANIZED NAILS: These zinc-coated nails are widely available. Hot-dipped galvanized (HDG) nails are more durable than electro-galvanized (EG) nails. But no galvanized nail provides lasting insurance against rust; the coating often flakes off.

ALUMINUM NAILS: Aluminum nails won't rust but aren't quite as strong as galvanized nails and can be difficult to drive (they bend). They are often used for siding.

STAINLESS-STEEL NAILS: These are rustproof, but they are costly and hard to find. They're durable and worth their expense for projects built near saltwater.

DRILLING PILOT HOLES FOR SCREWS

Screw Diameter	Pilot-Hole Diameter
4	$1/16$"
6	$3/32$"
8	$7/64$"
10	$1/8$"
12	$9/64$"
14	$5/32$"

Drill through the top piece into the bottom piece to a depth equal to the screw length. Clamp or hold the parts together as you drive the screw.

PREDRILLING FOR FASTENERS

When a nail or screw splits a board, it not only renders the board unsightly but takes away almost all of the fastener's holding power. Avoid both problems by drilling pilot holes wherever there is a possibility of splitting—especially close to the end of a board.

When attaching hardwood trim, drill a pilot hole for every nail. Use a drill bit that's slightly smaller than the nail. Test by drilling a hole and putting the nail in; it should be snug enough that you can't push the nail through with your finger.

For attaching softwood trim, try this trick: Insert the finishing nail in the chuck of your drill. Drill through the trim with the nail until it contacts the framing, then finish driving the nail with a hammer.

The chart at left shows pilot-hole sizes for screws.

SCREWS

Screws hold better than nails. The best ones to use for outdoor projects are decking screws—generally in $2\frac{1}{2}$- to $3\frac{1}{2}$-inch lengths. Deck screws are coated for weather resistance. With a cordless drill, you can drive these sharp, self-sinking screws about as fast as you can drive nails.

When driving screws within 2 inches of the end of a board, predrill pilot holes to keep the wood from splitting. (See the chart above for pilot-hole sizes.)

Match your screwdriver bit to the heads of the screws used. Decking screws generally have a phillips head. Some have a square-recess head or one that takes either a phillips or square-drive screwdriver tip. A phillips tip often cams out of a combination head under the torque of a cordless drill, especially when fastening 2× framing. If your phillips tip slips out of combination-head screws, switch to a square tip.

WHICH FASTENER?

For most projects nails are the least expensive fastener. Screws cost more, but they create a stronger joint, which can mean a longer-lasting structure. And even though driving an individual screw may take slightly longer than driving in a nail, screws save you time in the long run by requiring fewer fasteners.

An air or power nailer makes nailing fast and easy and is well worth the cost of the rental fee for a large project. Practice on scrap before starting work on your project. (See page 79 for more about power nailers.)

LAG SCREWS

A lag screw is a hex-head bolt with a wood-screw thread, usually $1/4$ inch or larger in diameter and up to 6 inches long. Lag screws are ideal for fastening heavy framing members and hardware. Predrill pilot holes for lag screws, then drive them with a wrench or, for more speed, a ratchet handle and socket.

BOLTS

Bolts, nuts, and washers provide a solid connection with excellent load-bearing strength. They hold parts together with

WHAT SIZE FASTENER?

The longer and thicker a nail is, the better it holds. However, a nail that's too thick for the stock (or is driven too close to the end) splits the wood which results in almost no holding power.

Although it might seem that a shed or gazebo calls for a wide selection of fasteners, those listed below will get you through most projects.
■ Common, spiral, or ringshank nails (10d or 16d) for framing with 2× or thicker stock
■ Box or ringshank nails (8d or 10d) for 1× or thinner stock
■ Finishing nails (8d or 10d) for trim
■ Decking screws (#10) in appropriate lengths
Refer to the "Nailing Schedule for Wood Framing" on page 70 to determine which nail sizes to use at framing joints.

FASTENERS
continued

compression. Size is designated by the shank diameter (under the head) and length. Use only those with a hot-dipped galvanized finish and predrill with a drill bit of the same diameter as the shank. The most common bolts for woodworking projects are machine bolts and carriage bolts.

Machine bolts have a hex or square head. Place washers under the head and nut, and use two wrenches to tighten machine bolts until they are just snug, making the slightest indentation in the surface of the wood. Carriage bolts have a rounded head with a square shank that pulls into the wood as the nut is tightened and keeps the bolt from turning. The round head gives a smooth, finished appearance.

MASONRY ANCHORS

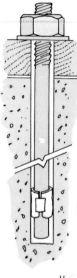

Anchor bolts expand against the concrete when the bolt is tightened. Drill a hole of the same diameter and at least ½" longer than the bolt. Blow the dust from the hole and drive in the bolt with the nut turned just to the top of the threads. Make sure the bolt doesn't turn when tightening.

Expansion shields have soft metal or plastic sides that expand as a screw or lag screw is tightened. Drill a hole of the same diameter and length, set the shield in the hole, and tighten the screw.

Hollow wall anchors are used to fasten lumber to hollow concrete blocks. Drill a hole of the same diameter into a block core, insert the anchor, and tighten the screw to draw the flanges against the inside wall of the block. Remove the screw, insert it through the material to be fastened, and retighten the screw in the anchor.

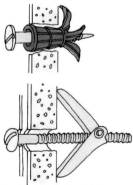

Also used to fasten material to concrete block, **toggle bolts** have wings that expand against the rear of a concrete surface. Drill a hole of the same diameter, insert the wings through the material to be fastened into the block, and tighten the bolt to flatten the wings against the block.

FRAMING CONNECTORS

Framing connectors are designed for special purposes. Those available from your distributor may not look exactly like the styles illustrated here.

Most manufacturers supply nails specially sized for framing connectors, but you can use common nails of the closest diameter, clinching the nail on back if it's longer than the framing.

MASONRY FASTENERS

Masonry fasteners are similar to nails or screws. Some are made of hardened steel and others rely on expansion and friction to grip masonry. The illustrations at left show some common installation methods.

NAILING SCHEDULE FOR WOOD FRAMING

Item	Method	Number	Size	Type
Band joist to joist	End	3	16d	Common
Band joist to sill	Toe	16" OC	10d	Common
Joist to sill	Toe	2	10d	Common
Bridging to joist	Toe	2	8d	Common
Ledger to beam	Face	³⁄₁₆" OC	16d	Common
Sole plate to stud	End	2	16d	Common
Top plate to stud	End	2	16d	Common
Stud to sole plate	Toe	4	8d	Common
Sole plate to joist	Face	16" OC	16d	Common
Doubled studs	Face	16" OC	10d	Common
Double top plate	Face	16" OC	10d	Common
Double header	Face	12" OC	12d	Common
Ceiling joist to top plate	Toe	3	8d	Common
Overlapping joists	Face	4	16d	Common
Rafter to top plate	Toe	2	8d	Common
Rafter to ceiling joist	Face	5	10d	Common
Rafter to hip rafter	Toe	3	10d	Common
Rafter to valley rafter	Toe	3	10d	Common
Ridge board to rafter	End	3	10d	Common
Rafter to rafter	Toe	4	8d	Common
Collar tie (2") to rafter	Face	2	12d	Common
Collar tie (1") to rafter	Face	3	8d	Common
Let-in brace to stud	Face	2 each	8d	Common
Corner stud to stud	Face	12" OC	16d	Common
Built-up beam (3 or 4)	Face	32" OC	20d	Common

FRAMING CONNECTORS

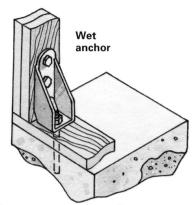

Wet anchor

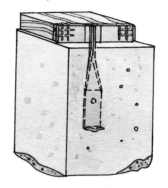

Heavy column base

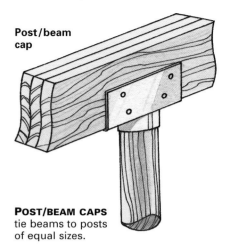

Post/beam cap

WET ANCHORS, a type of post connector, are inserted into a concrete foundation, slab, or post footing while the concrete is still wet.

HEAVY COLUMN BASES, also post anchors, are inserted into wet concrete.

POST/BEAM CAPS tie beams to posts of equal sizes.

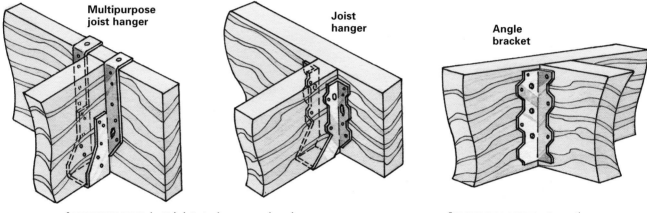

Multipurpose joist hanger

Joist hanger

Angle bracket

JOIST HANGERS butt joists to beams or headers. Single and double sizes are available.

ANGLE BRACKETS strengthen perpendicular joints—at rim joists and stair stringers, for example.

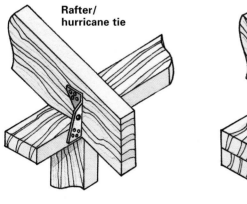

Rafter/ hurricane tie

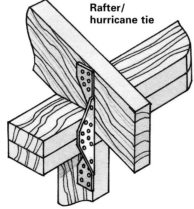

Rafter/ hurricane tie

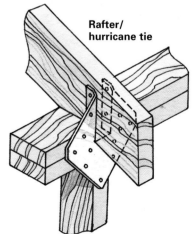

Rafter/ hurricane tie

RAFTER/HURRICANE TIES connect rafters to top plates.

Measuring, Marking, and Leveling

Taking Inside and Outside Measurements

OUTSIDE MEASUREMENT

Marking for Crosscuts

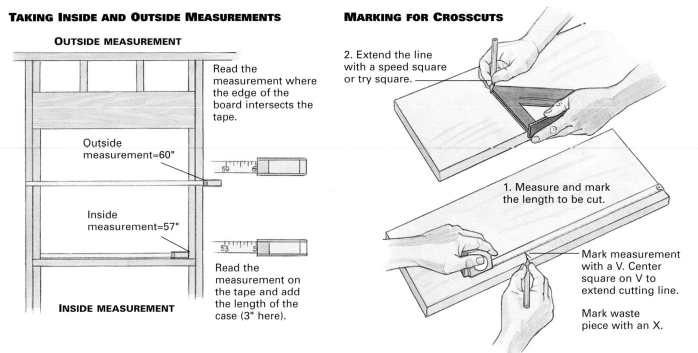

Read the measurement where the edge of the board intersects the tape.

Outside measurement=60"

Inside measurement=57"

Read the measurement on the tape and add the length of the case (3" here).

INSIDE MEASUREMENT

2. Extend the line with a speed square or try square.

1. Measure and mark the length to be cut.

Mark measurement with a V. Center square on V to extend cutting line.

Mark waste piece with an X.

Measuring and leveling are fundamental to construction. Complex calculations or expensive equipment are rarely required, but common sense and concentration always are. For accurate results and to avoid constant frustration, develop consistent habits. Jot down measurements on a piece of paper or on the wood you're measuring. Check boards for level at several points along their lengths before fastening them. Double-check measurements before cutting pieces or fastening them together.

TAPE-MEASURE TRAINING

Accurate measurements depend on a quality, easy-to-read tape measure. Buy a 25-foot model with a 1-inch blade and a blade lock. A 1-inch blade extends over long distances without buckling, making measurements easier. The blade lock keeps the tape extended so you can repeat measurements or reposition the hook if it slips off the end of a board.

Even if you've used a tape measure a few times, familiarize yourself with its features. The hook slides back and forth to compensate for its thickness. It slides out when making an exterior measurement and pushes in when making an inside measurement.

A blade that's divided into thirty-seconds of an inch for the first few inches is nice but not necessary. Carpentry rarely calls for measurements finer than $\frac{1}{16}$ inch.

Learn to spot the $\frac{1}{4}$- and $\frac{1}{8}$-inch markings when you look at the tape. They are good benchmarks for quickly recognizing measurements to the nearest $\frac{1}{4}$ or $\frac{1}{8}$ inch plus or minus the next $\frac{1}{16}$ inch. That way you don't have to count the number of sixteenths of an inch. For example, a measurement of $12\frac{13}{16}$ inches is easy to remember as $12\frac{3}{4}$ inches plus the next $\frac{1}{16}$ inch.

MARKING FOR RIP CUTS

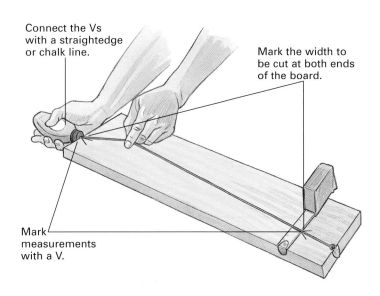

Connect the Vs with a straightedge or chalk line.

Mark the width to be cut at both ends of the board.

Mark measurements with a V.

USING A POST LEVEL

A post level checks for plumb on three planes. Hold the level on the post and adjust it until all three bubbles are centered in the vials.

USING A CARPENTER'S LEVEL

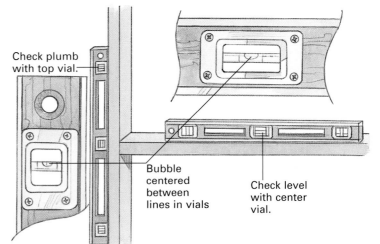

Check plumb with top vial.

Bubble centered between lines in vials

Check level with center vial.

Use the same tape throughout the project. Not all tapes measure exactly the same; some differ as much as ⅛ inch.

TAPE TIPS

■ Make sure the hook—not the grommet that holds the hook—has caught the board.
■ Use a sharp pencil.
■ Mark the cut line with a V, the waste side with an X. Position the saw with the kerf on the waste side so the width of the blade doesn't shorten your finished board.
■ When crosscutting a board into several pieces, mark and cut one piece at a time. Repeated cuts marked before cutting shorten the board.
■ Mark cuts in sheet goods with a chalk line.
■ Don't use your tape as a straightedge.
■ Always read the tape right side up.

LONG-DISTANCE LEVELING

When leveling objects that stand about 6 feet apart, you can use a line level hooked to a tightly stretched mason's cord. But even over short distances (especially on a windy day) a line level won't always give you the most accurate results. A water level offers an accurate low-cost way to level over long distances.

Operating on the principle that water seeks its own level in a closed system, the level consists of two clear plastic tubes that attach to both ends of a garden hose. Fill the level with water, place the ends on the objects to be leveled, and mark them, as shown at right. Some water levels sound a tone to indicate level. Water levels are available at hardware stores, home centers, and lumberyards.

Another option is to rent a surveyor's transit or a builder's level. Home centers and tool-rental dealers usually have them available. Some use a laser to mark a point, others employ small telescopes mounted on tripods. Both levels are designed to help you mark a spot on a pole. Renting this survey equipment usually costs more than buying a simple water level.

Water level here will be the same here.

CUTTING WITH A CIRCULAR SAW

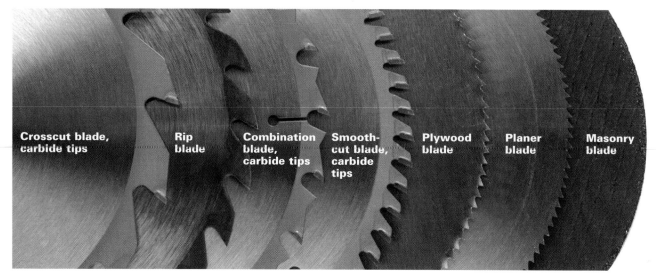

Crosscut blade, carbide tips | Rip blade | Combination blade, carbide tips | Smooth-cut blade, carbide tips | Plywood blade | Planer blade | Masonry blade

The portable circular saw is a basic carpentry tool. It cuts wood on-site with speed and efficiency—and with only a small sacrifice in precision. You can achieve accurate cuts by using the right blades and commercial or homemade cutting guides.

BUYING A CIRCULAR SAW

If you don't have a circular saw, buy one with a 7¼-inch blade and a motor rated at 10 to 13 amps. This is large enough and has enough power to cut through 2× stock at a 45-degree angle. Buy one that feels comfortable in your hand. Although you may be tempted to get a cordless saw, buy a corded saw and make a cordless drill your second purchase. An extension cord conveniently brings the power for the saw to the site, and you won't be slowed down by having to change and charge batteries.

COMMON CUTS

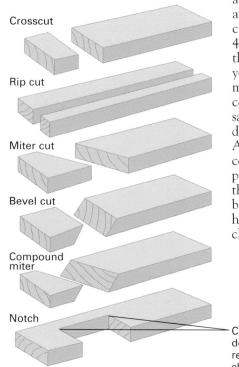

Crosscut

Rip cut

Miter cut

Bevel cut

Compound miter

Notch

Cut ends of notch to depth with handsaw, remove waste with chisel.

CHOOSING SAW BLADES

Ripping and crosscutting tears through wood fibers from different directions, so each ideally calls for a different blade. But the 18- to 24-tooth combination blade that comes with most saws makes both cuts adequately. (For smoother crosscuts in trim, you can buy a crosscut or planer blade.)

Buy carbide-tipped blades whenever possible. They long outlast carbon steel blades and are well worth the additional cost. You don't necessarily need to buy a premium-grade carbide blade. Midprice blades last a long time, and replacing an inexpensive blade may prove less expensive than sharpening a top-of-the-line blade.

SETUP AND PREPARATION

It takes about a minute to prepare for a circular saw cut. The first steps are to adequately support the board and align the blade correctly.

SUPPORTING THE WORKPIECE: By supporting the stock correctly, you'll not only reduce the chance of binding the blade, you'll also make cleaner cuts. Support the work on sawhorses or a stable work surface. If the waste side of the cut will be short, support the board on the nonwaste side, and let the waste fall away when the cut is completed.

If the waste side is long, its weight will cause the board to splinter and crack near the end of the cut. Support the work with two scrap pieces under each side, with the middle supports close enough to the center to keep

CROSSCUTTING WITH A CIRCULAR SAW

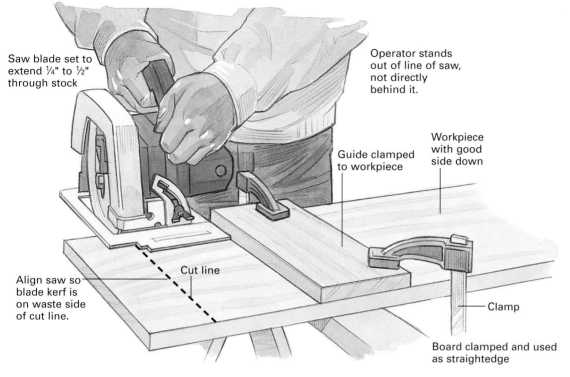

Saw blade set to extend ¼" to ½" through stock

Operator stands out of line of saw, not directly behind it.

Guide clamped to workpiece

Workpiece with good side down

Align saw so blade kerf is on waste side of cut line.

Cut line

Clamp

Board clamped and used as straightedge

the board from bending under the weight of the saw.

ADJUSTING THE BLADE: The bevel gauge on your saw may not be precise. To accurately square up the blade, unplug the saw and turn it upside down. Retract the guard, and hold a speed square against the blade (between two teeth) and the plate. Adjust the bevel gauge so the blade lines up with the square. Test your adjustment by cutting through a piece of 2× lumber.

MAINTAINING YOUR BLADES

Blades don't require much attention until they become dull. A few simple practices reduce your sharpening chores.

■ Store blades in commercial storage units or homemade dowel racks with spacers. Blades stacked on a workbench dull quickly; the metal surfaces wear and the edges of the teeth break.

■ Clean the pitch off your blades regularly. Pitch, resin or sap, that hardens on the blade increases friction and heat. Clean your blades with commercial pitch remover or oven cleaner, but don't use abrasives— they scratch the blade's surface and make subsequent pitch removal more difficult.

■ Sharpen your blades when they become dull. Burning, slow cuts, or a blade that feels like it's climbing out of the kerf are signs the blade needs attention. You can sharpen blades yourself, but sharpening is precision work best left to a local sharpening service.

CHANGING THE BLADE

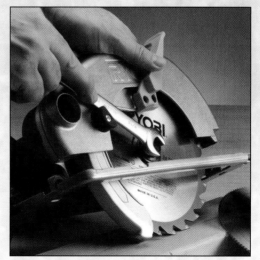

Before changing a circular saw blade, make sure the saw is unplugged. Retract the blade guard and set the teeth firmly into a piece of scrap. Remove the fastener with a wrench, and slide out the blade.

CUTTING WITH A CIRCULAR SAW
continued

RIP-CUTTING WITH A CIRCULAR SAW

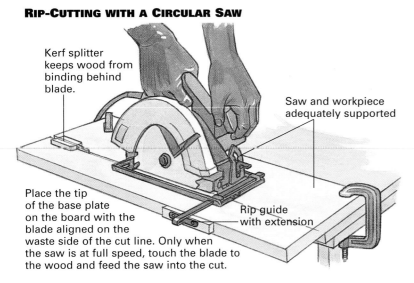

Kerf splitter keeps wood from binding behind blade.

Saw and workpiece adequately supported

Place the tip of the base plate on the board with the blade aligned on the waste side of the cut line. Only when the saw is at full speed, touch the blade to the wood and feed the saw into the cut.

Rip guide with extension

Flip over one of the two resulting pieces, and press one cut edge against the other cut edge. If the blade is square, they will line up perfectly. Scratch a new 90-degree mark on the bevel gauge so you will be able to adjust it quickly in the future.

SET THE CUTTING DEPTH: Allow the blade to extend ¼ inch (or three teeth) past

MAKING MITER CUTS

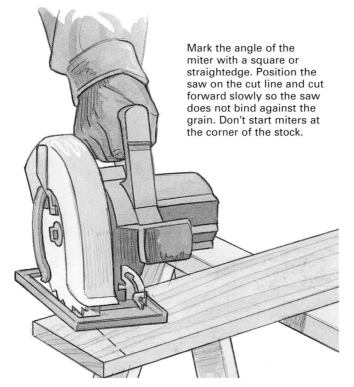

Mark the angle of the miter with a square or straightedge. Position the saw on the cut line and cut forward slowly so the saw does not bind against the grain. Don't start miters at the corner of the stock.

the thickness of the stock. Keeping three teeth out of the wood minimizes heat, reduces kickback, and keeps the blade free of sawdust. Become familiar with the kerf—the width of the cut—of your saw blade. An average blade removes about ⅛ inch. A plywood blade removes less, a carbide-tipped blade removes more.

MAKING THE CUT

Methods for making the most common cuts are illustrated on this page. Follow these tips to make all your cuts smooth and accurate.

KEEP THE GOOD SIDE DOWN: A circular saw cuts upward, splintering the upper face of the board. Therefore, when cutting trim, keep the side that will be visible down. Framing cuts need not be as precise.

START RIGHT: Place the saw plate on the work and line up the blade on the waste side of the cut line. Keep a firm grip on the saw and stand to one side of it as you turn it on and feed it into the work at a speed that allows the blade to cut freely. Feed speed varies depending on the kind of material being cut and its thickness.

Don't cut too slowly or make little turns to keep the blade near the cut line—you'll end up with a gaping, wavy cut line. Instead develop a smooth, fairly rapid forward movement that doesn't require a lot of force.

Keep the base plate resting on the board until the cut is completed. Then release the trigger and wait for the blade to stop spinning before lifting the saw.

KEEP THE CUT LINE IN SIGHT: Some carpenters align the cut line with the saw's sighting notch as they cut; others prefer to sight along the blade. For cuts that must be dead-on, sight the cut with the blade. When making long cuts where a straight cut is more important than an accurate cut, use the notch. For example, when cutting underlayment or plywood marked with a chalk line, use the notch as your visual guide.

USE GUIDES: Guides keep the saw blade straight in the kerf, which results in more accurate cuts and keeps the blade from binding. The simplest guide for crosscuts is a speed square. Start the cut, slide the square into place against the saw's base plate, and finish the cut. For a more secure guide, start the cut and stop the saw; square up and clamp

CUTTING BEVELS

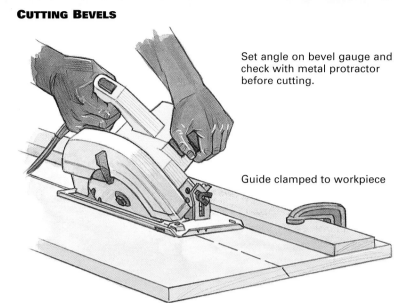

Set angle on bevel gauge and check with metal protractor before cutting.

Guide clamped to workpiece

a short board along the base plate, then finish the cut.

Most circular saws come with a rip fence, a metal guide that fastens to the base plate. This guide enables you to cut a fairly straight line parallel to the board's edge, as long as the piece to be cut is not too wide.

If the board is too wide to use a rip fence or if you're making long cuts on sheet goods, clamp a guide in place. You can make a two-piece jig or use a single straight board. Measure the distance between the outside edge of the base plate and the saw blade, and clamp the guide the same distance from the cut line. Be careful to keep the kerf to the waste side of the cut.

When making freehand cuts, be sure to rest your work on a steady base. Hold the workpiece firmly or clamp it to the work supports. With practice you'll be able to make accurate freehand cutoffs.

CUT THE STOCK, NOT THE CORD: Always make sure the cord is completely out of the blade's path. Do not splice a cut cord; replace it.

CUTTING THICK STOCK

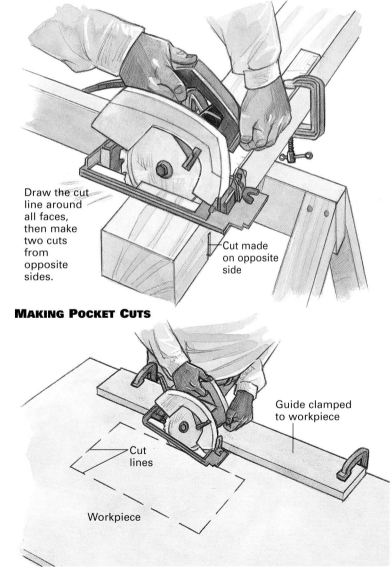

Draw the cut line around all faces, then make two cuts from opposite sides.

Cut made on opposite side

MAKING POCKET CUTS

Guide clamped to workpiece

Cut lines

Workpiece

MINIMIZING KICKBACK

When the teeth on the rear of the blade catch on a board, a saw kicks back, out of its cut line, ruining the cut and endangering the carpenter. Here's how to avoid kickbacks:

■ Don't try to change directions mid-cut. If your cut veers off the cut line, stop the saw, back up, and start again. Don't run the saw as you back it up—that also causes kickback.

■ Keep your blades sharp. If you have to push hard to make a cut, chances of kickback multiply.

■ Be sure to support the work securely. If the board bends down in the middle or if a heavy piece of waste falls away, it may grab the blade.

■ Sometimes a twisted board, or one with twisted grain, grabs the blade suddenly. Be prepared for this.

■ Never wear long sleeves or other clothing that could come near the blade as you cut. Never bring your face close to the blade as you cut. Keep the power cord clear of the cutting area.

Retract blade guard and rest saw plate on surface with blade on cut line. Turn saw on and gradually lower blade into work until saw plate rests on work. Move the saw forward. Finish corners with a handsaw or jigsaw.

FASTENING

FACE-NAILING

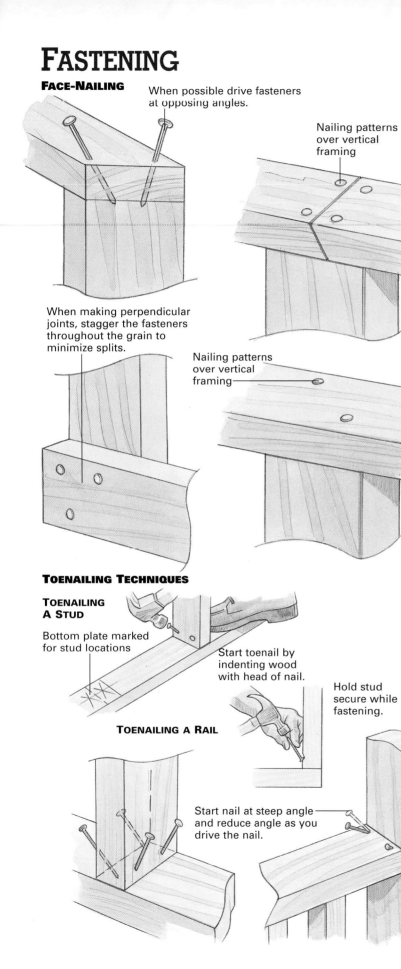

When possible drive fasteners at opposing angles.

Nailing patterns over vertical framing

When making perpendicular joints, stagger the fasteners throughout the grain to minimize splits.

Nailing patterns over vertical framing

TOENAILING TECHNIQUES

TOENAILING A STUD

Bottom plate marked for stud locations

Start toenail by indenting wood with head of nail.

Hold stud secure while fastening.

TOENAILING A RAIL

Start nail at steep angle and reduce angle as you drive the nail.

A good hammer for nails and a drill/driver for screws are two tools that will help you complete the project more smoothly and enjoyably.

For framing use at least a 20-ounce framing hammer. The heft of a 20-ounce hammer drives nails with much less effort than a lighter carpenter's hammer, making the work go faster and reducing fatigue. Switch to a lighter carpenter's hammer for trim work.

A cordless drill/driver with an 18-volt or larger battery has the power and battery life required for 2× framing. Buy a drill/driver with two batteries and keep one in the charger while you work with the other.

DRIVING NAILS

Here are some hints for better hammering.
TECHNIQUE: Hold the nail near the head and push it into the wood. Tap the nail until it stands in the wood by itself. Then let go and drive the nail home. Swing your arm instead of hammering from the wrist. A relaxed grip on the handle results in better aim. Keep your eye on the nailhead; dented boards are almost impossible to fix.
SETTING NAILS: Drive framing nails so the last blow sinks the head slightly into the surface without denting the wood. For a finished look on visible surfaces, drive a finishing nail nearly flush. Then set it with a nail set, fill the indentation with wood putty, and sand smooth.

USING A NAIL SET

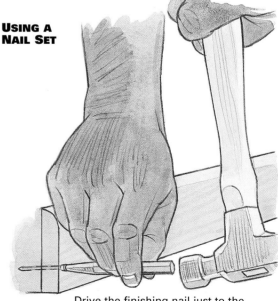

Drive the finishing nail just to the surface. Drive nailhead about ⅛" below surface of wood with a nailset.

**BLIND-NAILING
BY HAND**

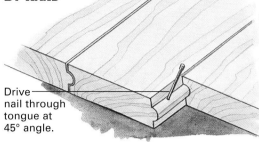

Drive nail through tongue at 45° angle.

DRIVING SCREWS

Although you may not need to predrill framing stock, predrilling is always a good thing to do when fastening trim. Predrilling avoids splits and reduces the tendency of the pieces to move as the screw penetrates.

TECHNIQUE: Set your drill/driver to low speed and set the clutch so it leaves the head slightly below the surface of the wood. You may need to experiment a few times to get the setting right. Hold the screw head on the driving tip and push it firmly with the drill when you start it. Start at a slow speed, then increase pressure and speed as the screw bites into the wood. Keep the pressure on until the clutch slips and the screw head sinks slightly into the wood.

FASTENER LENGTH

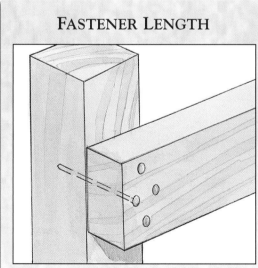

Carpenters use different rules of thumb for determining the length of fasteners. Some say a fastener should be about three times longer than the thickness of the top board. With ³⁄₄-inch stock, however, that risks a 2¹⁄₄-inch fastener poking through a 2×4. To be safe choose fasteners that penetrate the bottom board to about two-thirds of its thickness.

BLIND-NAILING WITH A FLOORING NAILER

A flooring nailer speeds installation of tongue-and-groove flooring and roofing. The tool forces the tongue-and-groove joint together as it drives a nail at the correct angle.

USING A POWER NAILER

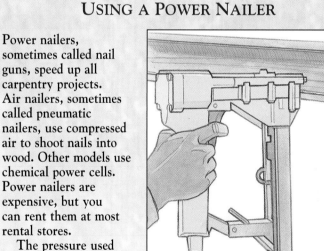

Power nailers, sometimes called nail guns, speed up all carpentry projects. Air nailers, sometimes called pneumatic nailers, use compressed air to shoot nails into wood. Other models use chemical power cells. Power nailers are expensive, but you can rent them at most rental stores.

The pressure used to drive the nails is adjustable, so you can set the tool to countersink nails or leave them flush with the surface. Here are some of the advantages nail guns offer over hand nailing.

■ The gun can be operated with one hand, leaving the other hand free to steady the work and keep it aligned.

■ A single blow drives the nail from the gun, eliminating the repeated hammer blows that can jolt a piece out of alignment.

■ The risk of bending a nail or missing the nailhead and damaging the workpiece is eliminated.

■ Nails used in nail guns are thin and have blunt tips that seldom split the workpiece.

LAYOUT AND FOUNDATION BASICS

LAYING OUT THE SITE

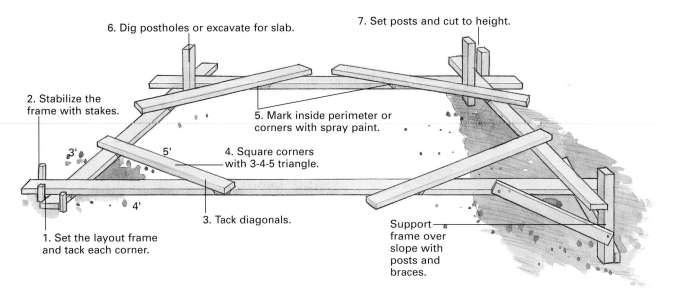

6. Dig postholes or excavate for slab.

7. Set posts and cut to height.

2. Stabilize the frame with stakes.

5. Mark inside perimeter or corners with spray paint.

3'

5'

4. Square corners with 3-4-5 triangle.

4'

3. Tack diagonals.

Support frame over slope with posts and braces.

1. Set the layout frame and tack each corner.

Accurate layout and a solid foundation ensure that your construction project proceeds smoothly and that your structure gives long, trouble-free service.

LAYOUT

The frame method described here is quicker and easier than setting up batter boards and lines. Use 14-foot 2×6s to lay out any size structure up to 12×12; use shorter or longer pieces if necessary. When you're done laying out the site, use the boards for joists or rafters. Here's how to lay out the site.

■ Overlap four 14-foot 2×6s to make a frame with interior dimensions the size of your structure. Tack each corner with one screw. Stabilize the frame with stakes.

■ Lay diagonal braces across the corners. Tack each on one end.

■ Mark 3 feet from the inside corner on one board, 4 feet on the other. Adjust the frame until the diagonal measurement between the marks is 5 feet. This squares the corners. Tack diagonals in place, maintaining the interior dimensions of the frame.

■ For a foundation excavation, mark the perimeter on the ground with spray paint. Remove the frame and excavate. For posts or piers, mark the corners on the ground and leave the frame in place.

■ Dig postholes to the depth required by local codes. Pour 6 inches of dry concrete mix into each hole and tamp.

■ Set the posts and tamp the soil around them with a 2×4. Plumb each post on both sides. Remove the frame and cut the posts with a reciprocating saw.

POST FOUNDATIONS

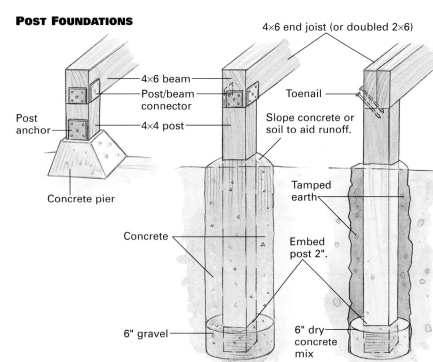

4×6 end joist (or doubled 2×6)

4×6 beam

Post/beam connector

Toenail

Post anchor

4×4 post

Slope concrete or soil to aid runoff.

Concrete pier

Tamped earth

Concrete

Embed post 2".

6" gravel

6" dry concrete mix

POURING A SLAB

4. Pour concrete.

5. Working in 5-foot sections, consolidate concrete with shovel or 2×4; tap forms to set concrete.

3. Set dobies and wire mesh (if local codes require).

6. Screed (level) with 2×4, using seesaw motion across surface.

2. Spread, level, and tamp gravel.

7. Finish the surface in sections immediately after screeding.

1. Lay out site, excavate, and stake 2× forms with cleats at joints.

POSTS AND SLABS

When it comes to the floor, you have two choices: a wood frame floor supported on posts or piers or a slab foundation. Check with your local building department about building codes and specifications to ensure that your foundation meets local requirements. Refer to the illustrations on these pages for installation methods and keep the following tips in mind.

■ For posts or piers premixed concrete is the most economical. For slabs less than 10×12 feet, consider mixing your own with a rented power mixer. For larger slabs ready-mix concrete is most cost-effective.

■ When pouring concrete, work from the far end of the forms toward the mixing site or ready-mix truck. If you're pouring ready-mix concrete, enlist a crew of two or three helpers.

■ Excavate for slabs to a depth that accommodates a 4- to 6-inch gravel base and 3 inches of concrete.

■ Make the slab forms the same height as the finished slab so the forms can serve as guides for screeding.

■ For posts use naturally resistant woods or treated lumber that's rated for ground contact.

■ Using your scaled plans, mark one post at the correct height, cut it with a reciprocating saw, and use a line or water level to mark and cut the remaining posts.

FINISHING THE SLAB

Float the slab

1. Level the surface with a bull float, keeping the leading edge raised slightly so it doesn't dig in. Then float with a darby.

Set anchor bolts or rebar

2. When the concrete stiffens, insert J bolts or other anchors where indicated on the forms. Leave enough thread for nuts.

Finish the surface

3. Steel troweling gives the concrete a smooth surface. Wait until the surface water disappears before troweling.

Cover slab

4. Prevent the concrete from drying too quickly while it cures. Plastic sheeting traps the moisture to control drying.

FRAMING THE FLOOR

Framing the floor of a small outdoor structure is relatively easy. Marking, cutting, squaring, and leveling the assembly creates a solid base for the walls and the roof. If the floor frame proves solid, strong, rigid, and square, the rest of the structure goes up with ease. The following methods for framing a floor are just two of many you can use.

TERMINOLOGY

Most floors have the same basic structural members.

JOISTS: horizontal flooring members set on edge to support the floor. Generally they run parallel to the short dimension of a structure, set either 16 or 24 inches on center. Such spacing allows the edges of standard 4×8 flooring to be centered on the joists.

HEADER: a member at the end of shortened joists to keep them vertical.

END JOISTS: joists attached to the headers at each end of the floor.

BEAM: a header on the long dimension of the frame.

FLOORING (or **decking**): fastened to the joists. (Called **subflooring** when used to support finished flooring.)

BLOCKING: 2× stock fastened within and perpendicular to the joists to keep them from twisting. Not usually necessary in small outdoor structures.

MUDSILL: attached to a concrete slab with J bolts or other anchors, it provides a nailing surface for framing on a slab.

FLOOR-FRAMING TIPS

To frame a shed floor, refer to the illustrations on these pages and follow the steps shown. (Refer to page 42 for gazebo framing). The additional tips here help keep everything straight.

■ Mark both headers at once to ensure that the joists run parallel to each other. If the distance between posts or the length of one side of the slab is longer than the other, make

TYPICAL FLOOR FRAMING

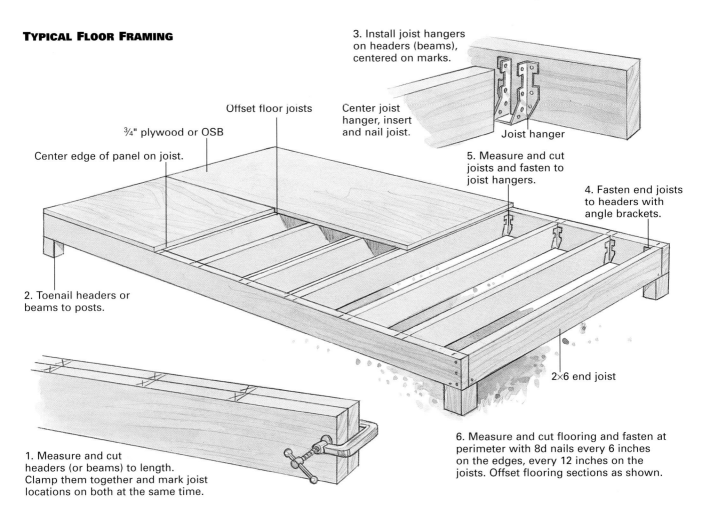

3. Install joist hangers on headers (beams), centered on marks.

Offset floor joists

Center joist hanger, insert and nail joist.

Joist hanger

¾" plywood or OSB

Center edge of panel on joist.

5. Measure and cut joists and fasten to joist hangers.

4. Fasten end joists to headers with angle brackets.

2. Toenail headers or beams to posts.

2×6 end joist

1. Measure and cut headers (or beams) to length. Clamp them together and mark joist locations on both at the same time.

6. Measure and cut flooring and fasten at perimeter with 8d nails every 6 inches on the edges, every 12 inches on the joists. Offset flooring sections as shown.

allowances and mark the headers together.

■ Measure all similar distances before cutting. Lumber, an imperfect product, will exhibit variances despite your best intentions. For example, measure the length of all joists before cutting the first one and write the result on the top of the header. If the measurements are the same, cut them all at one time. If each measurement is different, cut them one at a time.

■ Center J bolts on the mudsill or 1¾ inches from the edge of a slab. They often end up, however, more or less removed from the edge. After scribing the sides of the bolt on the sill, mark their positions from the edge before drilling the sill.

■ Use full-length boards where possible. Structural splicing should not be necessary for small outdoor structures.

■ Use pressure-treated lumber for all floor framing members, and plywood or OSB rated for flooring and exterior use (⅝" or ¾" stock is typical).

■ If building a structure larger than the dimensions in this book, install a central beam supported by a center post, or consult span tables and adjust the size of the joists (see "How Far Can Joists Span?" on page 67).

■ Check all corners for square with a framing square and adjust framing as you fasten it.

■ Snap chalk lines on the flooring at 16- or 24-inch intervals to keep the nails centered in the joists.

■ Though plywood and OSB expand very little, leave a ⅛-inch space between each sheet to avoid compression buckling. Use an 8d nail to get the right spacing.

DECKING PATTERNS

The framing methods shown at right accommodate both parallel and diagonal decking patterns. Other decking patterns require additional support which can be added to the basic parallel-joist construction. Whatever pattern you choose, plan the framing before you start, making sure it is adequately supported at the ends.

FRAMING A FLOOR ON A SLAB

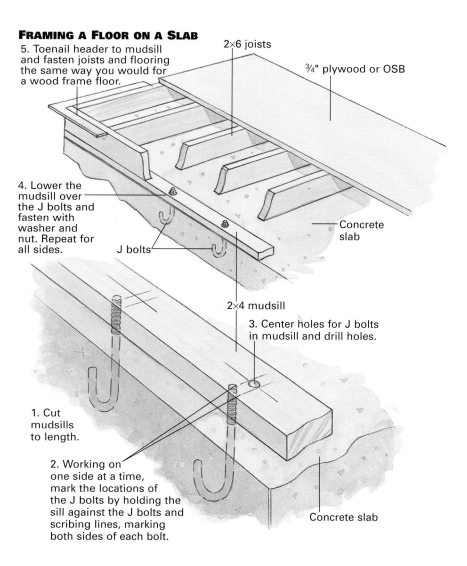

5. Toenail header to mudsill and fasten joists and flooring the same way you would for a wood frame floor.

2×6 joists

¾" plywood or OSB

4. Lower the mudsill over the J bolts and fasten with washer and nut. Repeat for all sides.

J bolts

Concrete slab

2×4 mudsill

3. Center holes for J bolts in mudsill and drill holes.

1. Cut mudsills to length.

2. Working on one side at a time, mark the locations of the J bolts by holding the sill against the J bolts and scribing lines, marking both sides of each bolt.

Concrete slab

DECKING PATTERNS

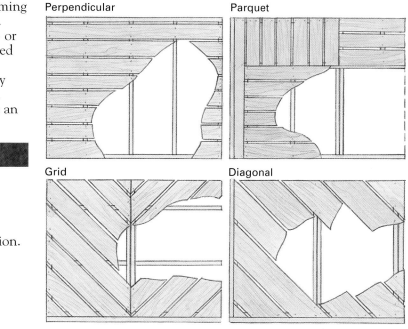

Perpendicular

Parquet

Grid

Diagonal

FRAMING A WALL

TYPICAL WALL FRAMING

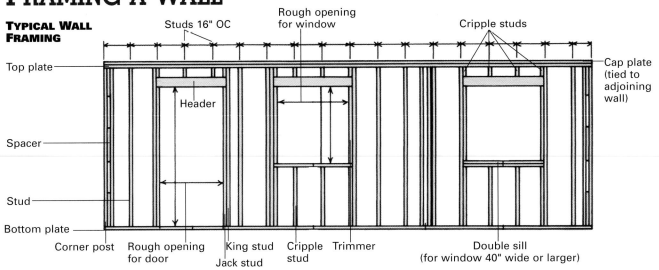

Studs 16" OC

Rough opening for window

Cripple studs

Top plate

Cap plate (tied to adjoining wall)

Header

Spacer

Stud

Bottom plate

Corner post   Rough opening for door   King stud   Cripple stud   Trimmer   Double sill (for window 40" wide or larger)

Jack stud

All frame walls consist of the same elements arranged in the same fashion. Differences arise primarily in the location of window and door openings.

ANATOMY OF A WALL

Before building your walls, familiarize yourself with their components.

STUDS: 2×4s spaced every 16 or 24 inches on center and fastened between top and bottom plates. Cut the studs 3 inches shorter than the height of the ceiling to account for the thickness of the top and bottom plates. Studs for an 8-foot (96-inch) unfinished ceiling would therefore be cut at 93 inches. When estimating, figure one stud for every lineal foot of wall. You'll cut up the extras for blocking and cripple studs. Use standard framing lumber for the framing; kiln-dried stock for door and window openings.

PLATES: dimension lumber the same size as the studs that support the bottoms of the studs and span their tops. An overlapping cap plate on top ties the walls together (see the illustration above).

OPENINGS: doors and windows are framed with a **header** (doubled 2× stock) across the top, supported by **jack studs** (also called shoulder studs) that run to the floor. Support the jack stud with a full-length stud at its side. **Cripple studs** fill in the opening at the top of doors and at the top and bottom of windows. Make sure the rough openings are about 1 inch wider than the frame of your window or door. It's better to have these units on-site so you can measure them before framing the walls.

LAYING OUT A WALL

Lay out the longest walls first, marking stud locations as shown in the illustration on the opposite page. Clamp together the top and bottom plates of each wall and mark the stud locations, as well as the locations for framing members for door and window openings.

If you're working in inches on center, begin at the end of the plates. If your marks represent the edges of the studs, tack a ¾-inch scrap on the end of the plates and measure from the inside of the scrap. This makes the first mark 14¼ inches from the end of the plates. Measure 16 inches thereafter.

ASSEMBLING A WALL

Assemble each wall as a separate unit, using the floor as a work surface. Build the corner posts first, face-nailing blocking between two studs. Assemble door and window openings with a header, king studs, trimmers, and sill, if needed. Lay these assemblies on the floor between the top and bottom plates and nail them through the plates at the marks with two 16d nails. Then face-nail the cripple studs from the plate, and toenail them into the header.

WALL LAYOUT (TOP VIEW)

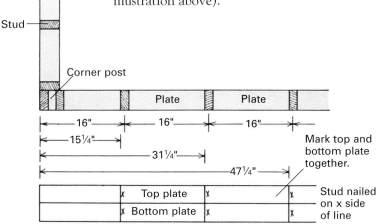

Stud

Corner post

Plate   Plate

16"   16"   16"

15¼"

31¼"

47¼"

Mark top and bottom plate together.

	Top plate		
x		x	x
x	Bottom plate	x	x

Stud nailed on x side of line

RAISING THE WALLS

Snap chalk lines on the floor to mark the inside edge of the bottom plates. Then, with the aid of a helper, lift the wall in place and nail it to the floor at every stud. Plumb the wall in both directions and brace it temporarily to the deck with 2×4s. Assemble, erect, and brace the adjoining wall. Measure and cut the cap plates and clamp the longest pair together, offsetting them by 3½ inches. Mark the locations of the rafters and nail the plates to the top plates, overlapping them at the corners to tie the walls together. Finish by installing sheathing.

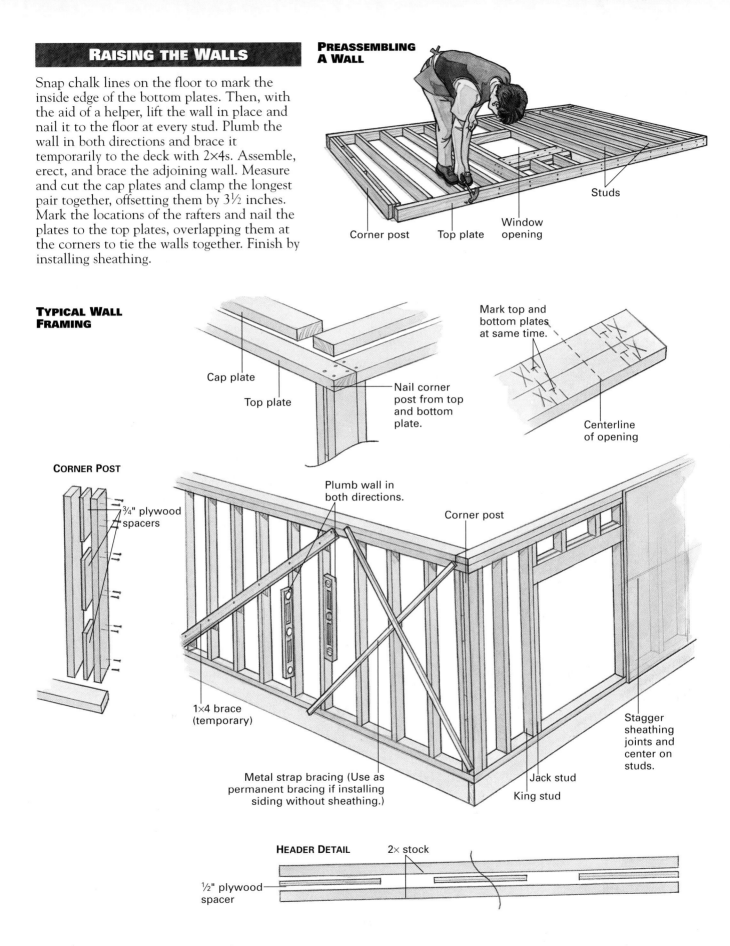

PREASSEMBLING A WALL

Corner post

Top plate

Window opening

Studs

TYPICAL WALL FRAMING

Cap plate

Top plate

Nail corner post from top and bottom plate.

Mark top and bottom plates at same time.

Centerline of opening

CORNER POST

¾" plywood spacers

Plumb wall in both directions.

Corner post

1×4 brace (temporary)

Metal strap bracing (Use as permanent bracing if installing siding without sheathing.)

King stud

Jack stud

Stagger sheathing joints and center on studs.

HEADER DETAIL

2× stock

½" plywood spacer

ROOF FRAMING

The way in which you frame the roof of your garden shed contributes more to the style of the structure than any other aspect of its construction. Although there are many different roof-framing styles, the three illustrated on these pages are easily adapted to almost any garden shed.

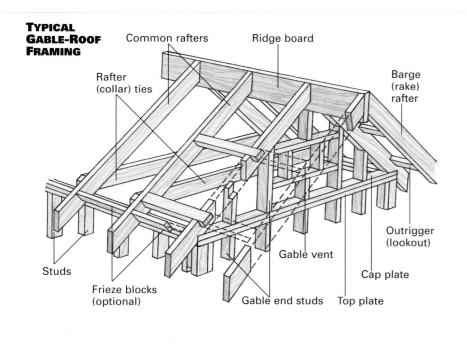

TYPICAL GABLE-ROOF FRAMING

Common rafters · Ridge board · Barge (rake) rafter · Rafter (collar) ties · Outrigger (lookout) · Studs · Frieze blocks (optional) · Gable vent · Gable end studs · Top plate · Cap plate

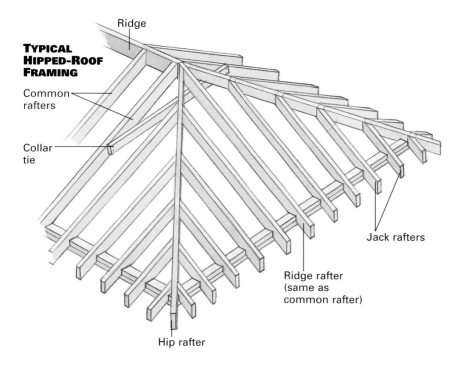

TYPICAL HIPPED-ROOF FRAMING

Ridge · Common rafters · Collar tie · Jack rafters · Ridge rafter (same as common rafter) · Hip rafter

ANATOMY OF A ROOF

For the average do-it-yourselfer, roof framing is often—but doesn't need to be—accompanied by a fair amount of anxiety. Like any other task, it pays to start by familiarizing yourself with the basic anatomies of each style. Each of them has the same common elements.

RIDGE BOARDS: stiffen the entire roof and provide a nailing surface for the rafters.

RAFTERS: the main support for the finished roof materials, rafters have different names depending on their position.

- **COMMON RAFTERS** extend from the ridge to the wall.
- **BARGE RAFTERS** (also called rake rafters or verge rafters) extend beyond the wall and overhang the rakes.
- **OUTRIGGERS** (or lookouts) are 2×4s notched into the last two common rafters on the rake to support the barge rafters.
- **HIP RAFTERS** (on a hipped roof) extend from the ridge to the corners of the wall.
- **JACK RAFTERS** extend from hip rafters to the wall.
- **VALLEY RAFTERS** attach an extended roof to the main roof.

RAFTER TIES (also called collar ties): span the shorter dimension of a structure and keep the weight of the roof from pushing out on the walls.

Notice that the framing beneath the rake (called the gable wall) is actually an extension of the lower wall and is framed with studs and a rough opening for the gable vent. Frame the gable wall after the roof is up, cutting and notching each stud to fit.

VOCABULARY OF A RAFTER

Each rafter is cut from a single board, but each cut has its own name and function.

RIDGE CUT (or plumb cut): determines the pitch of the roof and fastens to the ridge board.

BIRD'S MOUTH: allows the rafter to fit squarely on the cap plate. Its **PLUMB CUT** is made at the same angle as the ridge cut. The **SEAT CUT**, at right angles to the plumb cut, rests on the cap plate.

RAFTER TAIL: extends beyond

the wall and terminates in a **TAIL CUT** made at the same angle as the ridge cut.

RISE, RUN, AND PITCH

Roofs need to slope in order to shed rain or snow, but the pitch of a roof (how much it slopes) also contributes greatly to its appearance. How you pitch the roof is largely a matter of aesthetics, but steeper roofs are more difficult to work on and require longer rafters and more roofing material. As a starting point, you may want to match the pitch of the roof on your house, especially if the shed lies close to the house.

Here's what you need to know before you lay out your rafters.
RISE: the distance from the top plate (or seat cut) to the center point on the ridge.
RUN: the distance from the outside edge of the wall (the edge of the cap plate or rafter plumb cut) to the midpoint of the ridge.
SPAN: the total distance from the outside edge of one wall (the cap plate) to the opposite wall.
SLOPE: how much the rafter rises for each foot of its run. Thus a roof with 6/12 pitch rises 6 inches for every foot of run.

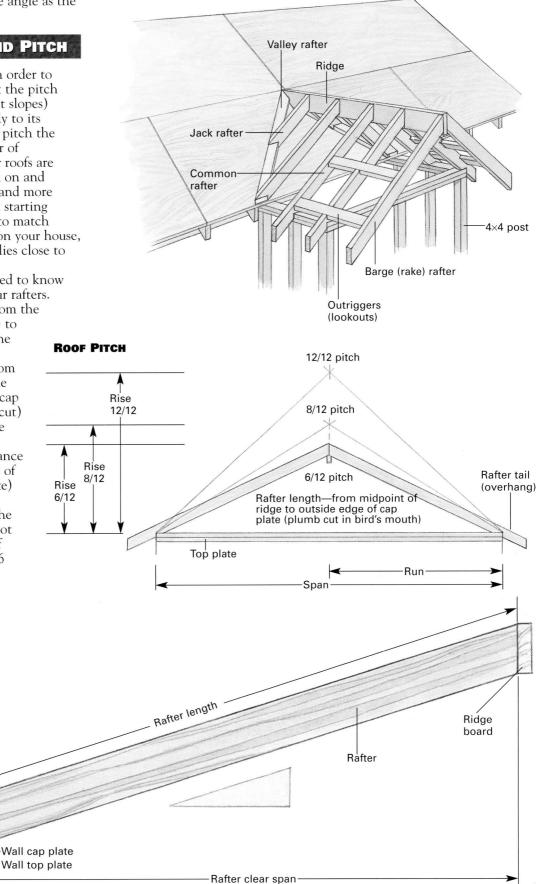

TYPICAL GABLE-ROOF EXTENSION

Valley rafter
Ridge
Jack rafter
Common rafter
4×4 post
Barge (rake) rafter
Outriggers (lookouts)

ROOF PITCH

Rise 12/12
Rise 8/12
Rise 6/12

12/12 pitch
8/12 pitch
6/12 pitch
Rafter tail (overhang)
Rafter length—from midpoint of ridge to outside edge of cap plate (plumb cut in bird's mouth)
Top plate
Run
Span

Rafter length
Ridge board
Rafter
Wall cap plate
Wall top plate
Rafter clear span

ROOF FRAMING
continued

PITCH AND ANGLE	
Pitch	**Angle**
12/12	45.0°
10/12	39.75°
8/12	33.75°
7/12	30.25°
6/12	26.5°
5/12	22.5°
4/12	18.5°

USING A FRAMING SQUARE

A framing square is a remarkable tool that combines a squaring tool and a calculator. With it, not only can you mark consistent perpendicular lines, you also can make other calculations critical to rafter layout.

Before you begin using the square, remember that the length of a rafter is the distance from the center of the ridge to the plumb cut of the bird's mouth—not the distance to the rafter tail.

The rafter scales are six rows of numbers along the middle of the square's body. The top shows the length of a common rafter per 12 inches of run. The inch marks above the rafter tables correspond to pitch. For example, the 6 represents a 6/12 pitch. The number in

the first row below the 6 is 13.42. This means that for a 6/12 pitch, each common rafter is 13.42 inches long for every 12 inches of run; 67.1 (67⅛) inches for a 5-foot run, for example.

At the same pitch, a hip rafter (the second line on the scale) would be 18 inches long for every foot of run. This is because a hip rafter slopes in two directions.

LAYING OUT RAFTERS

No matter what kind of roof you're constructing, lay out rafters in this order:
■ Position the framing square with the rise and run intersecting the bottom of the rafter.
■ Mark all plumb cuts: ridge cut, bird's mouth, and tail.
■ Mark the seat cut 3½ inches long at a right angle to the bird's-mouth plumb cut.
■ Reposition the square at the same numbers back one-half the thickness of the ridge from the first line, and mark the ridge cut.

CUTTING RAFTERS

Keep these tips in mind when cutting rafters:
■ Make all cuts for common rafters 90 degrees to the face of the board.
■ Hip and jack rafters extend two directions from the ridge, so the ridge cut is a compound miter. Refer to the illustration on the opposite page, and make these cuts with a compound miter saw.

RAFTER SCALES

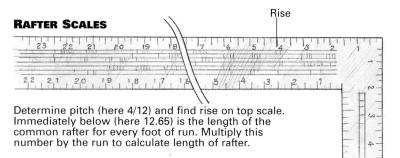

Determine pitch (here 4/12) and find rise on top scale. Immediately below (here 12.65) is the length of the common rafter for every foot of run. Multiply this number by the run to calculate length of rafter.

CUTTING COMMON RAFTERS

1. Place square on rafter so the rise (here 4") and the run (12 for common rafters) intersect with the bottom of the rafter. Mark the plumb cut line.

2. Determine rafter length from framing square and mark it on the top of the board. Extend the mark to the bottom of the board.

3. Reposition the square on the mark and scribe bird's-mouth plumb cut.

4. Position the blade perpendicular to the bird's-mouth plumb cut until the tongue is 3½" from the bottom of the board. Mark the seat cut.

5. Measure from the bottom of the bird's-mouth to the length of the rafter tail (overhang), and mark the tail cut.

6. Mark a line parallel to the ridge cut and half the thickness of the ridge board. Cut here and at all other lines.

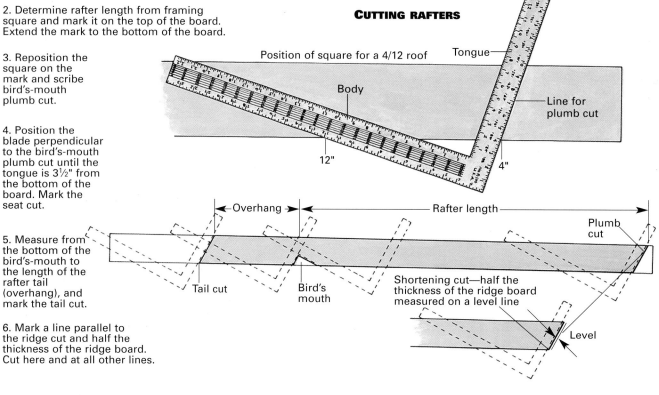

CUTTING RAFTERS

Position of square for a 4/12 roof

Tongue

Body

Line for plumb cut

12"   4"

Overhang — Rafter length — Plumb cut

Tail cut   Bird's mouth

Shortening cut—half the thickness of the ridge board measured on a level line

Level

CUTTING HIP RAFTERS

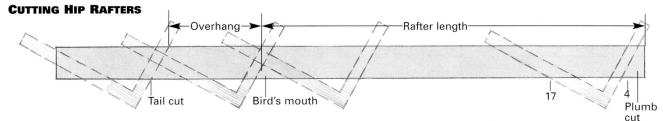

1. Position framing square with rise (here 4 inches) and run (17 for hip rafters) intersecting the bottom of the board.

2. Mark and make all cuts as you would a common rafter, shortening plumb cut and cutting it as a compound miter.

HIP-RAFTER MITERS

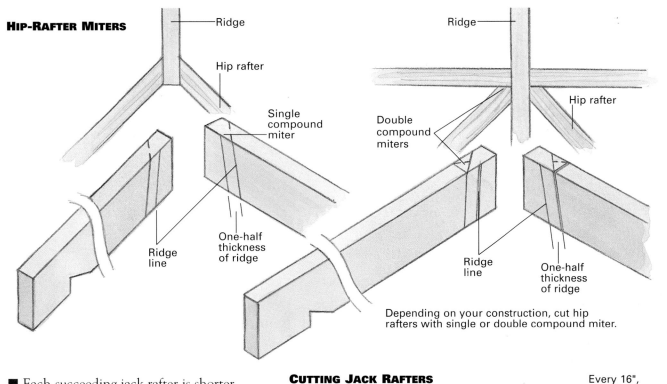

Depending on your construction, cut hip rafters with single or double compound miter.

■ Each succeeding jack rafter is shorter than the previous one, working down the hip rafter. This difference is consistent with the pitch of the roof. The third scale on the framing square shows how much shorter each rafter is.

Jack rafters are cut with left and right miters, depending on which side of the hip rafter they are on. Mark each one before you cut it.

INSTALLING RAFTERS

Mark the ridge board for the locations of the rafters. Cut the ridge to length and raise it into place with temporary bracing. After you've cut the first common rafter, test-fit it and make adjustments. Then cut the remaining common rafters to the same dimensions. Fasten the common rafters at the marks on the ridge and cap plates. Then install hip and jack rafters on a hipped roof. Fasten collar ties at each rafter, if necessary.

CUTTING JACK RAFTERS

Compound miter

Every 16", rafters will be shorter by the same amount, their common difference in length

16" OC

1. Using roof pitch from your dimensioned plan (here 4/12) and third scale on framing square, determine how much shorter each succeeding jack rafter will be (here 16.87") with rafters set 16" OC.

2. Lay out each jack rafter with the same methods used for a common rafter, shortening each rafter by the common difference.

3. Cut each rafter to length, keeping those with left and right compound miters separate.

INSTALLING COMPOSITION SHINGLES

style and manufacturer, three or four bundles cover a square.

All composition shingles have strips of roofing cement just above the tabs. When the shingles are installed, the sun heats the cement (even in the winter) and bonds the shingles together, making them extremely unlikely to blow off.

SHINGLING A GABLE ROOF

Shingling a roof begins with fastening the decking—¾-inch exterior-grade plywood or OSB—to the rafters. It's much like laying flooring at an angle. Sheathing a roof, however, is best done with a helper.

INSTALL SHEATHING: Start with a full panel and slide it up the ladder and on the roof. On roofs with shallow pitches, the decking might stay in place, but it's wise to have one person hold it temporarily with a notched 2×4. Position the panel flush with the outside edge of the rake rafters and square to the top of the rafter tails, and nail it with 8d nails every 12 inches on the perimeter, 8 inches on the rafters. Cut the remaining pieces and install them, offsetting the joints and spacing them at ⅛-inch.

EDGE THE EAVES: Drip edging keeps rain off the edges of the sheathing and helps prevent rot. Nail P-shaped drip edging to the eaves (not the rakes) with steel or aluminum nails, the same metal as the drip edge.

INSTALL UNDERLAYMENT: Underlayment is asphalt-impregnated paper (often called roofing felt) that provides a second layer of protection. Use 15-pound underlayment for composition shingles. Fasten the first row of underlayment with five or six staples squared to one of the bottom corners of the roof. Unroll the paper to the other side, pull tight, cut it flush with the rake, and staple it. Keep the paper straight along the eave.

Staple the second and succeeding courses in the same fashion, overlapping each one by 6 inches. Lay paper across the top of the ridge and staple it after laying the underlayment on the other side. At valleys and hips, and on gazebo roofs, carry the paper at least 18 inches past the joint.

FLASH THE VALLEYS: (You need to do this only on roofs with dormers or extensions.) Center a sheet of underlayment on the

C omposition shingles cover more roofs in the United States than any other material.

Once made from asphalt and paper, composition shingles are now manufactured with a core of cellulose or fiberglass fibers that's coated with asphalt on both sides. Even the least expensive shingles have a 20-year warranty and a Class A fire rating. They come in many colors to match or complement your outdoor structure. Some even look like wood shingles and slate.

Three-tab composition shingles are the easiest to install. Usually 12 inches deep and 36 inches long, they are packaged in bundles and sold by the square (enough shingles to cover 100 square feet). Depending on the

INSTALLING COMPOSITION SHINGLES

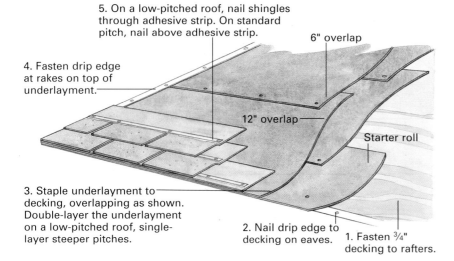

5. On a low-pitched roof, nail shingles through adhesive strip. On standard pitch, nail above adhesive strip.

6" overlap

4. Fasten drip edge at rakes on top of underlayment.

12" overlap

Starter roll

3. Staple underlayment to decking, overlapping as shown. Double-layer the underlayment on a low-pitched roof, single-layer steeper pitches.

2. Nail drip edge to decking on eaves.

1. Fasten ¾" decking to rafters.

valley and staple it as shown in the illustration below.

EDGE THE RAKES: Nail drip edge to the rakes.

INSTALL THE STARTER STRIP: Like other courses, the starter strip needs to provide an adhesive for the next course. You can install shingles with the tabs pointing up or use starter roll made for this purpose (it's faster and less expensive). Overhang the starter strip on the drip edge by ¼ inch.

INSTALL THE FIRST COURSE: Snap a chalk line along the length of the roof at the depth of the shingle, minus ¼ inch. Line up a full shingle on the chalk line, flush with the rake edge. Nail it just below the adhesive strip with two nails per inch from each end and one above each tab.

Fasten shingles as far as you can reach, keeping them lined up on the chalk line. If you installed upside-down shingles for a starter course, put a dab of roofing cement under each corner of the shingles. Then start the second course.

INSTALL THE REMAINING COURSES: After the first course is laid, offset the next course by 4, 5, or 6 inches. The illustration at top right shows a 5-inch offset, a pattern very forgiving of discrepancies.

To run a 5-inch offset quickly, align the first shingle of the second course on the preceding row, offsetting it with a 5-inch piece of ¼-inch plywood lined up with the edge of the first corner shingle.

Keeping the alignment straight, cut the shingle flush with the rake drip edge with a hooked roofer's utility knife, and nail it. Use the same procedure to offset each successive course until you have laid the seven courses.

Start the eighth course with a full shingle and continue to the ridge. Always start at the rake with an uncut shingle. Work in sections as far as you can comfortably reach, then move across the length of the roof. If you're right-handed you'll probably find it more comfortable to start from the lower left-hand corner and work up and to the right.

At the ridge, cut the shingles so they don't overlap the other side.

INSTALL THE RIDGE SHINGLES: Make ridge shingles by cutting the tabs off a full shingle. Starting at the end of the ridge that faces the direction of the prevailing winds, nail down the first ridge shingle, overlap and nail the next one, and continue to the other end of the ridge.

LAYING A 5-INCH OFFSET PATTERN

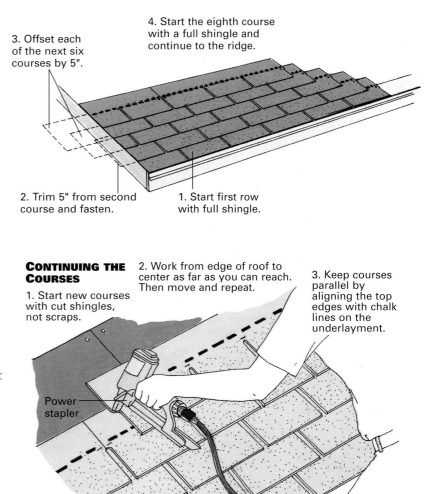

3. Offset each of the next six courses by 5".

4. Start the eighth course with a full shingle and continue to the ridge.

2. Trim 5" from second course and fasten.

1. Start first row with full shingle.

CONTINUING THE COURSES

1. Start new courses with cut shingles, not scraps.

2. Work from edge of roof to center as far as you can reach. Then move and repeat.

3. Keep courses parallel by aligning the top edges with chalk lines on the underlayment.

Power stapler

LAYING A CLOSED VALLEY

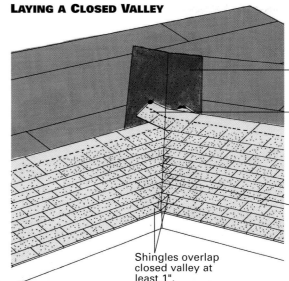

1. Flash the valley; center a full sheet of roll roofing there. Staple it over underlayment.

2. Fasten shingles in the pattern of your choice, extending the valley shingles of alternate courses over the adjoining roof by at least 12".

3. Keep shingle nails at least 6" away from valley seam.

Shingles overlap closed valley at least 1".

INSTALLING COMPOSITION SHINGLES
continued

SHINGLING A HIPPED ROOF

Shingling a hipped roof requires more cutting than a gable roof but is an otherwise similar job. Start in the lower left corner (or the opposite for lefties) of one of the sides and place the starter strip and first course as you would on a gable roof, staggering the pattern.

Cut the shingles at the hip so they don't overlap the adjoining roof. Center the cut on the hip, leaving less than ¼ inch between the shingles on each side.

Offset the second course as outlined for a gable roof. Finish adjoining sections, then shingle the hips the same way.

Refer to the illustrations below, keeping the following tips in mind.

HIP SHINGLES: You can buy hip shingles or cut your own from full shingles. When cutting your own, trim the heel of the shingle narrower than the tab so the edges of the heel won't show.

To guide the placement of the hip shingles, temporarily tack a hip shingle at the top and snap a chalk line between the top and bottom shingles along one edge. Remove the top shingle.

RIDGE SHINGLES: Start ridge shingles at each end of the ridge and work toward the center. Nail a shingle at each end and snap a chalk line between them to guide the placement of the remaining shingles.

At the center, trim the final shingles to fit. Then trim the tab off a shingle and cap the joint with the tab. Nail at each corner and cover the nailheads with caulk or roof cement.

DON'T LET THE NAILS SHOW

The ideal roofing nail for the job is just long enough to pass through the layers of shingles and stop just short of piercing the roof deck. If the fasteners completely pass through the roof deck, they will show through and will quickly rust from condensed moisture.

If you install regular single-ply shingles on a new ¾-inch plywood roof deck, use ¾-inch nails. If, for a finished ceiling, you install 2× roof decking or 1× tongue-and-groove decking with ¾-inch decking over it, you can use longer nails.

SHINGLING THE HIPS AND RIDGES

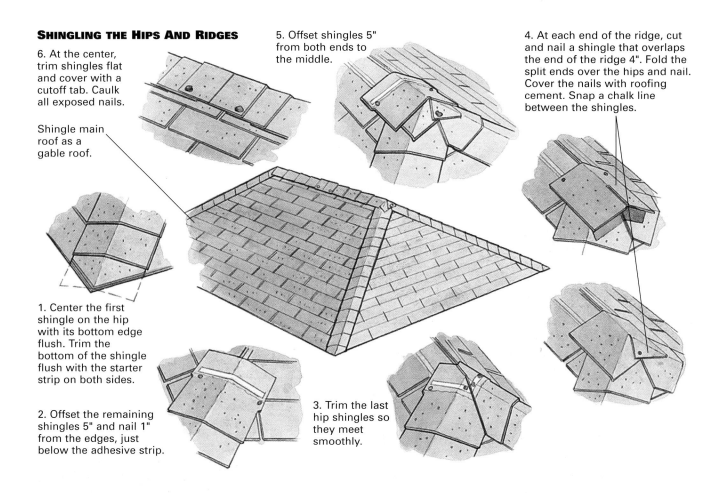

6. At the center, trim shingles flat and cover with a cutoff tab. Caulk all exposed nails.

Shingle main roof as a gable roof.

5. Offset shingles 5" from both ends to the middle.

4. At each end of the ridge, cut and nail a shingle that overlaps the end of the ridge 4". Fold the split ends over the hips and nail. Cover the nails with roofing cement. Snap a chalk line between the shingles.

1. Center the first shingle on the hip with its bottom edge flush. Trim the bottom of the shingle flush with the starter strip on both sides.

2. Offset the remaining shingles 5" and nail 1" from the edges, just below the adhesive strip.

3. Trim the last hip shingles so they meet smoothly.

SHINGLING A DORMER OR ROOF EXTENSION

As you shingle the main roof, carry the courses toward the ridge and the dormer or extension. If you have a dormer, extend the courses below it from one side to the other.

When you reach the rear of the eave of the dormer or extension, shingle the extended roof with the same offset and exposure as the main roof, letting alternate courses extend a foot across the valley. Then bring over the next courses of the main roof and finish the valley, letting alternate courses extend by a foot.

Before you carry the main roof shingles above the dormer ridge, shingle the dormer ridge, starting from the outer edge and working toward the main roof.

When you get to the main roof, split the top of the last shingle and carry it at least 4 inches up the main roof. Lap the shingles coming across on the main roof over the last shingle of the extension ridge. Neatly trim the main roof shingles around the dormer ridge shingles.

Carry the course immediately in line with the top of the dormer roof at least 10 feet beyond the right side. Nail only the tops of these shingles. You will later slip the preceding course under this one.

Continue roofing above this line to the ridge. Now, using the cutouts above and below the course you extended to the right

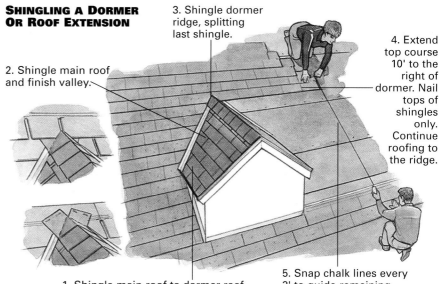

SHINGLING A DORMER OR ROOF EXTENSION

3. Shingle dormer ridge, splitting last shingle.

2. Shingle main roof and finish valley.

4. Extend top course 10' to the right of dormer. Nail tops of shingles only. Continue roofing to the ridge.

1. Shingle main roof to dormer roof edge, then shingle roof extension, extending alternate courses across the valley.

5. Snap chalk lines every 3' to guide remaining shingles and finish roof.

of the dormer, snap a chalk line from the ridge to the eave near the right edge of the dormer. Snap succeeding lines at 3-foot intervals (the length of a shingle). Then finish shingling the main roof, sliding the last course under the top one.

LOADING A ROOF

Have your roofing delivered to the rooftop of your shed, especially if the shed is large. Many dealers will stock the roofing on the roof for a slight extra charge. Composition shingles weigh about 80 pounds per bundle; it's a lot easier to have your supplier hoist them up for you.

If your order is too small to warrant the supplier delivering it with a hoist, or if the supplier does not have the equipment, cut the bundle wrapping and take about half a bundle up the ladder at a time. Having the roofing on the roof puts it within easier reach and saves you time. Once you begin roofing, you won't want to go down the ladder and bring up more supplies.

DON'T FALL OFF

Roofing jacks (sometimes called roof brackets or toe-board jacks) are metal straps that hold a plank that acts as a foothold on a steep roof. You can walk back and forth on the roof, putting part of your weight on the board.

Nail the roofing jacks securely to the roof with regular 16d nails driven through the notched bracket into a rafter. Always drive the nails where they will be covered by a subsequent course of shingles. When it's time to move up the jack, tap the bottom with a hammer to free it from the nail, then pound the exposed nail into the roof deck rather than pull it.

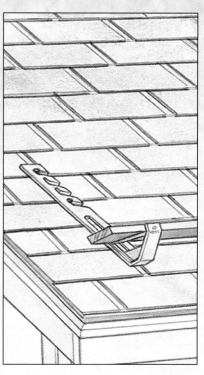

INSTALLING WOOD SHINGLES AND SHAKES

Wood shingles are smaller and lighter than shakes and are usually sawn smooth on both sides. Shakes are split rather than sawn, which gives them a rougher appearance. Both are made from western red cedar.

Wood shakes and shingles are installed in much the same way, but each has its own look. Shakes look more rugged; shingles, more orderly.

CHARACTERISTICS OF SHAKES AND SHINGLES

Wood shingles are sawn on both sides. Shakes may be split (taper-split), sawn (taper-sawn), or split on one side and sawn on the other (hand-split and resawn).

Shakes and shingles are graded No. 1 (the best), No. 2, and No. 3. For sheds and other secondary buildings or for siding, use No. 2 treated or untreated grade. Treated stock often lasts longer than 30 years.

Shingles and shakes are sold in bundles, with four to seven bundles per square (100 square feet). They are cut in 15-inch lengths for the starter course and in 16-, 18-, and 24-inch lengths for finished courses. Each length has a maximum exposure—the amount of shingle showing—but you can install them with shorter exposures to create a different look. Shingle exposures are shown on the chart on the opposite page.

GENERAL GUIDELINES

Wood shakes and shingles are installed like composition shingles, with these differences:
■ Install untreated shingles and shakes over spaced 1×4s to allow air to circulate. Shakes and treated shingles can be installed over plywood sheathing, but shakes require underlayment between the rows, no matter what the sheathing. In areas with wind-driven snow, use solid sheathing and treated stock.
■ Metal drip edges are not used with wooden shingles and shakes. Instead overhang the first course by 1½ inches.
■ Use galvanized nails or aluminum staples with a minimum 7⁄16-inch crown in a pneumatic stapler. Put one fastener about an inch in from each edge and about 2 inches above the exposure. With a 5-inch exposure, for instance, you would nail about 7 inches up from the bottom edge of the shingle. See the chart on page 96 for fastener lengths.

INSTALLING SHEATHING

■ Install open sheathing for sawn shingles to allow air circulation. To keep 1×4s spaced consistently, place a short piece of scrap wood between the boards.
■ Sheath the top 18 inches of the roof solidly so you can adjust the exposure to make the last course come out even at the ridge.
■ Install sheet sheathing as you would a floor, spacing the sheets at ⅛ inch and offsetting the joints.

INSTALLING UNDERLAYMENT

■ Use 30-pound felt paper.
■ When installing shakes, install an 18-inch-wide layer of felt paper between the courses as you go (see illustration, opposite middle). Nail the top edge of this underlayment just enough to hold it straight; the subsequent courses will secure it.

SHEATHING THE ROOF (SPACED SHEATHING FOR SHINGLES)

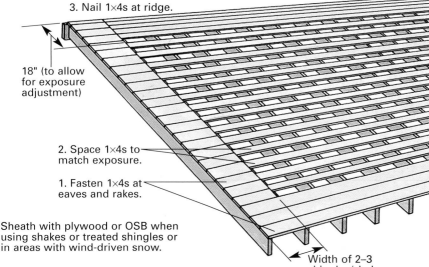

3. Nail 1×4s at ridge.

18" (to allow for exposure adjustment)

2. Space 1×4s to match exposure.

1. Fasten 1×4s at eaves and rakes.

Sheath with plywood or OSB when using shakes or treated shingles or in areas with wind-driven snow.

Width of 2–3 shingles/shakes

If you can't buy 18-inch-wide felt in your area, cut a roll in half by cutting around it with a circular saw with an old blade. You may have to finish the cut with a handsaw.

■ On hipped roofs and gazebos, overlap the underlayment by at least 18 inches, weaving alternate layers from one side to the other.

LAYING THE COURSES

■ Place shingles with straight, smooth edges at the rake.

■ Apply the first course directly over the starter course.

■ Maintain a consistent exposure for each course. Use a roofer's hatchet or cut a piece of ¼-inch plywood to the length of your exposure and use it to space the courses.

■ To ensure that your courses remain straight, measure up from the butts of the shakes at each end of the roof—every three or four courses up—and snap a chalk line as a guideline for the next course.

■ Maintain a ¼-inch spacing between each shingle or shake to allow for expansion. Offset the spacing 1½ inches from shingles in the preceding course. In addition make sure no joint is directly above another joint two courses below.

ROOFER'S HATCHET

A roofer's hatchet is a must when roofing with cedar shakes and shingles. That's because you don't cut shakes and shingles—you split them. The roofer's hatchet offers two other handy tools:

■ AN EXPOSURE GAUGE: A knob fits into a hole in the blade to gauge the shingle exposure.

■ A COMPOSITE SHINGLE CUTTER: The cutting blade is replaceable or can be sharpened.

MAXIMUM EXPOSURE

Length	Exposure
16"	5"
18"	5½"
24"	7½"

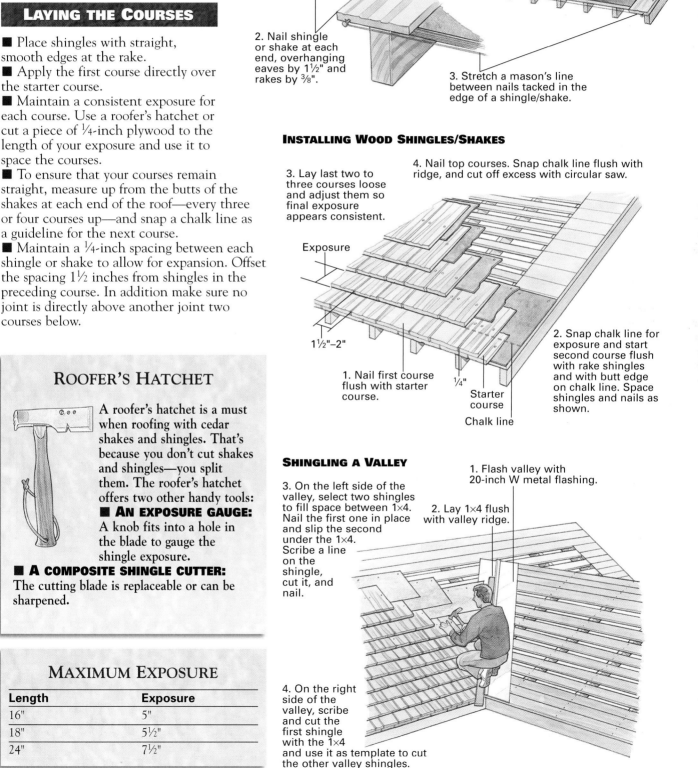

LAYING UNDERLAYMENT AND STARTER COURSE

1. Staple full-width 30-lb. felt paper flush with eaves and rakes.

For shakes and treated shingles on solid sheathing, continue underlayment to ridge.

2. Nail shingle or shake at each end, overhanging eaves by 1½" and rakes by ⅜".

3. Stretch a mason's line between nails tacked in the edge of a shingle/shake.

INSTALLING WOOD SHINGLES/SHAKES

3. Lay last two to three courses loose and adjust them so final exposure appears consistent.

4. Nail top courses. Snap chalk line flush with ridge, and cut off excess with circular saw.

Exposure

1½"-2"

1. Nail first course flush with starter course.

¼"

Starter course

Chalk line

2. Snap chalk line for exposure and start second course flush with rake shingles and with butt edge on chalk line. Space shingles and nails as shown.

SHINGLING A VALLEY

3. On the left side of the valley, select two shingles to fill space between 1×4. Nail the first one in place and slip the second under the 1×4. Scribe a line on the shingle, cut it, and nail.

1. Flash valley with 20-inch W metal flashing.

2. Lay 1×4 flush with valley ridge.

4. On the right side of the valley, scribe and cut the first shingle with the 1×4 and use it as template to cut the other valley shingles.

INSTALLING WOOD SHINGLES AND SHAKES
continued

■ Shingles and shakes are not uniform in width—minimize trimming by trying different shingles instead of cutting.
■ If a shingle or shake splits as you nail it, consider it two shakes and put a nail on each side of the split.
■ Cut shingles and shakes with a jigsaw around obstacles, a circular saw at valleys.

VALLEYS

To cut valley shingles in advance, find several wide shingles. Lay one under the 1×4 spacer (see illustration, page 95), score it, and cut it. Use this one as a template for cutting the remaining shakes and shingles.

As you approach the valley, put a precut shingle up against the 1×4, then find one or more shakes or shingles that will fit. You may have to split one of the fill-in shakes or shingles to get it to fit just right, but that's usually easier than cutting all the valley shingles individually.

SHINGLING HIPS AND RIDGES

Shakes and shingles for ridges and hips are factory-made to form a V. Each one has a seam in its crown; the seams must alternate going up the hip or across the ridge for maximum protection.
■ Nail hip and ridge shingles and shakes with nails long enough to penetrate the deck at least ½ inch—usually ½ inch longer than the nails used for the rest of the roof.
■ As with valleys, shakes or shingles running up the left side of a hip must be cut as you reach the hip. On the right side, cut the bottom shake or shingle at the proper angle and use it as a pattern to cut the rest.
■ Apply a double hip shake or shingle at the eave. For a smooth fit, cut the starter one even with the bottom of the second course, as shown at left. Apply the first hip shingle or shake over that, and continue up the hip.
■ Trim the inner edges of the hip shingles or shakes where they meet each other, then trim the tops flush with the ridge.
■ Next to a vertical wall, such as along a dormer, install step flashing.

SHINGLING A HIP

Nail above exposure.

5. Trim wood hip shingles/shakes at top as you would trim composition shingles.

4. Nail succeeding shingles, alternating direction of overlap.

3. Nail second shingle flush with the first.

2. Cut bottom shingle even with starter shingle. Nail shingles at the bottom and top (temporarily), and snap a chalk line between them.

1. Cut starter shingle to conform to angle of the hip.

INSTALLING WOOD SHINGLES AND SHAKES ON A RIDGE

1. Nail ridge shakes at both ends of the ridge and snap a chalk line between them.

3. Continue nailing across the ridge.

2. Starting at the end of the ridge that is away from prevailing winds, nail a shingle/shake over the first one.

4. Remove the shingle used for the chalk line and nail final shingle.

SHINGLE AND SHAKE NAILS

Type of Shingle/Shake	Minimum Length
15", 16", or 18" shingles	1¼" (3d)
24" shingles	1½" (4d)
18" or 24" hand-split and resawn	2" (6d)
18" or 24" taper-sawn	2" (6d)
18" or 24" taper-split	1¾" (5d)

INSTALLING A STEEL PANEL ROOF

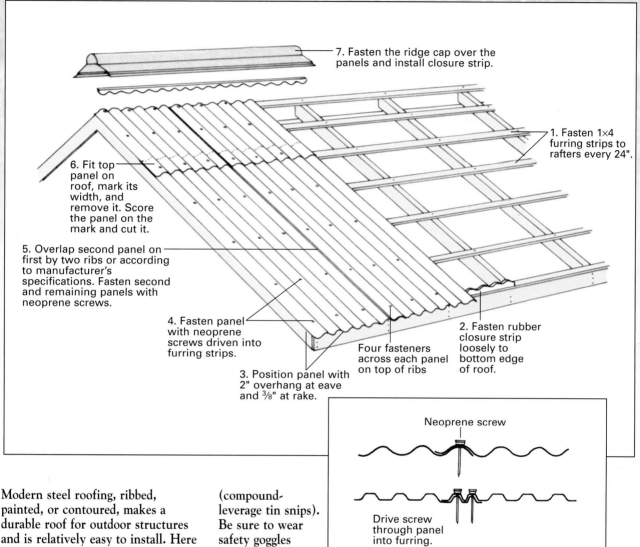

7. Fasten the ridge cap over the panels and install closure strip.

1. Fasten 1×4 furring strips to rafters every 24".

6. Fit top panel on roof, mark its width, and remove it. Score the panel on the mark and cut it.

5. Overlap second panel on first by two ribs or according to manufacturer's specifications. Fasten second and remaining panels with neoprene screws.

4. Fasten panel with neoprene screws driven into furring strips.

2. Fasten rubber closure strip loosely to bottom edge of roof.

Four fasteners across each panel on top of ribs

3. Position panel with 2" overhang at eave and ⅜" at rake.

Neoprene screw

Drive screw through panel into furring.

Modern steel roofing, ribbed, painted, or contoured, makes a durable roof for outdoor structures and is relatively easy to install. Here are some general tips to guide you.
■ Panels come in 39- and 26-inch widths, so allow for some overlap; actual coverage is 36 or 24 inches. Most panels are custom-cut at the factory at little or no charge. Be sure your measurements are precise.
■ When a roof requires more than one panel from eave to ridge, order long and short pieces and overlap them. The overlap should be about 12 inches, with longer laps—about 18 inches—on lower-pitched roofs.
■ The edges of metal panels are sharp. Always wear gloves and don't let people work directly below you.
■ Cut panels with a carbide steel blade in a circular saw. Special roller cutters work well on steel panels. Make small cuts with aviation snips

(compound-leverage tin snips). Be sure to wear safety goggles when cutting.
■ Fasten panels with panel screws made for this purpose. These screws have a sharp tip and self-tapping threads that penetrate the panel and are fitted with a rubber seal.
■ Drive screws on top of a ridge, not in a valley, where more water flows. Seat the washer firmly against—but do not dent—the panel. Drive fasteners about every 6 inches (depending on the pattern and the manufacturer's recommendation) from side to side, every 2 feet.
■ Matching accessories for valleys, rakes, eaves, and ridges are available for most styles of roof panels. They provide a better seal as well as a uniform look.

■ Install the first panel perfectly straight. All others interlock, and if the job starts out crooked you have little room to make adjustments in subsequent courses.
■ For added protection on low-pitched roofs, place a thick bead of caulk under the bottom edge of the overlapping panel.
■ Install the factory-supplied ridge caps to match your roof panel style. They overlap each other by 12 inches and are fastened to the roof the same way panels are.

INSTALLING SIDING

Siding comes in a wide range of materials. Here is a brief survey of popular siding.

WOOD SIDING

PANEL SIDING: Plywood panel siding is durable and extremely strong. Available in 4×8, 4×9, and 4×10 sheets with redwood, cedar, and less expensive veneers, its styles include smooth and rough finishes and grooved patterns that imitate board siding.

Use ⅜" (smooth) or ⅝" (grooved) exterior-grade siding, and paint or stain it. Install structurally rated siding directly on studs.

SOLID WOOD: Milled from lumber, board siding often comes with special edges or profiles. If made from cedar or redwood, or treated with a preservative, solid wood siding can last 50 years or longer. Redwood, cedar, and cypress weather to a silver gray if untreated. They can be stained and finished to a rich array of colors.

ORIENTED STRAND BOARD (OSB): OSB is not as strong or durable as plywood, but it has the advantage of being molded to look like clapboard siding. It ordinarily comes factory-primed, and you must reprime and paint it after installation.

SHINGLES AND SHAKES: The relatively high cost of cedar shakes and shingles is offset by several factors. You can install them yourself, they're attractive, they don't need painting or staining (although you can do either), and they last for many years. Both are sold unfinished or preprimed. Also available

are 4×8-foot panels with wood shingles already attached. These panels are installed like panel siding but look like regular shingles. Buy No. 2 shingles and if untreated, apply preservative yourself.

OTHER SIDING

You can side an outdoor structure with any of the same siding you can use on a house—fiber cement panels, metal and vinyl sidings stucco, and any number of masonry surfaces. Some of these materials are made to approximate the appearance of wood products. All will provide long-lasting results. Choose your siding with design features and maintenance requirements in mind.

INSTALLING PANEL SIDING

■ Panel siding is heavy and awkward, so have helpers on hand for the job.
■ Plan the installation to make joints as inconspicuous as possible. Leave a ⅛-inch gap between edges of plain siding, ¼ inch at openings. Cover plain joints with battens.
■ Keep bottom edge 8 inches above grade.
■ Use 6d aluminum or stainless-steel siding nails or hot-dipped galvanized nails. Nail at 6-inch intervals along the edge, 12-inches in the sheet.
■ At gables cut the panel to the angle of the roof pitch (see table, page 88). Fit the panel to the gable, trimming from the bottom.
■ At openings install the panel first. Drill holes at the corners of the opening, snap chalk lines between the corners, and cut the openings with a jigsaw or circular saw.
■ Caulk the gap at openings and where panels meet at the corners.
■ Trim outside corners with a 1×3 on one side and a 1×4 on the other. Extend top window trim across the side trim.

VERTICAL SIDING

Vertical siding boards are usually ¾ inch thick and range in width from 3½ to 11¼ inches.
■ Install vertical siding over studs with horizontal blocking every 2 feet.
■ Start vertical siding at the lowest corner of the structure. Plumb the first boards with a 4-foot level even if the structure is not plumb. Hide out-of-square corners with trim.
■ For tongue-and-groove siding, install groove-side interior to wall. Tap succeeding boards in place, with scrap to protect the tongue.

PROFILES OF PANEL SIDING

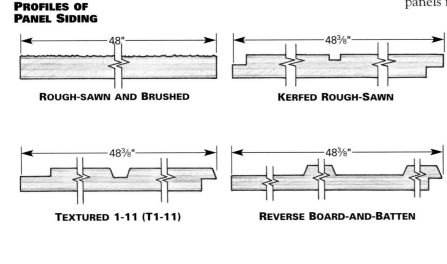

ROUGH-SAWN AND BRUSHED — 48"

KERFED ROUGH-SAWN — 48⅜"

TEXTURED 1-11 (T1-11) — 48⅜"

REVERSE BOARD-AND-BATTEN — 48⅜"

CHANNEL GROOVE — 48⅜"

INSTALLING PANEL SIDING

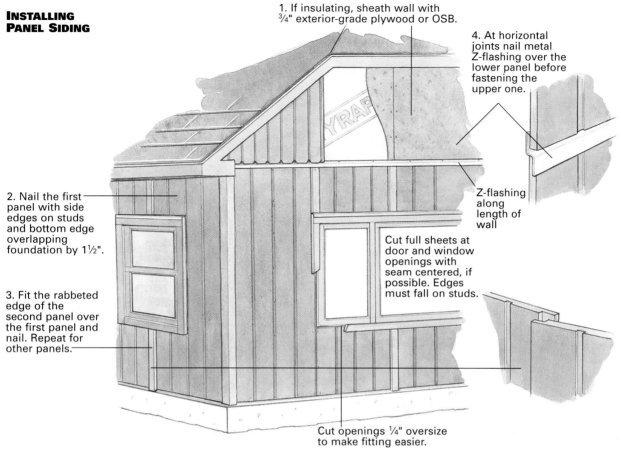

1. If insulating, sheath wall with ¾" exterior-grade plywood or OSB.

4. At horizontal joints nail metal Z-flashing over the lower panel before fastening the upper one.

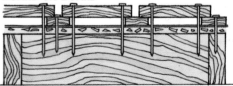

Z-flashing along length of wall

2. Nail the first panel with side edges on studs and bottom edge overlapping foundation by 1½".

3. Fit the rabbeted edge of the second panel over the first panel and nail. Repeat for other panels.

Cut full sheets at door and window openings with seam centered, if possible. Edges must fall on studs.

Cut openings ¼" oversize to make fitting easier.

TRIMMING CORNERS AND WINDOWS

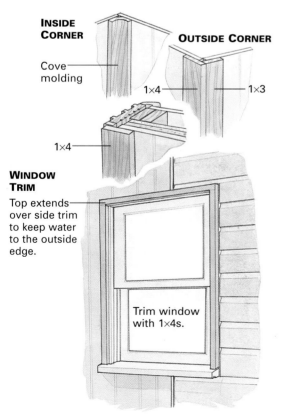

INSIDE CORNER

Cove molding

OUTSIDE CORNER

1×4   1×3

1×4

WINDOW TRIM

Top extends over side trim to keep water to the outside edge.

Trim window with 1×4s.

PROFILES OF VERTICAL SIDING

1. Sheath structure with plywood or OSB.

2. Nail first bottom board; plumb with 4' level.

3. Nail succeeding bottom boards, leaving ¼" gap.

4. Nail battens or top boards.

BOARD-AND-BATTEN

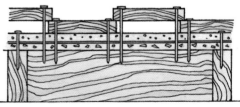

BOARD-ON-BOARD

REVERSE BOARD-AND-BATTEN

CHANNEL SHIPLAP

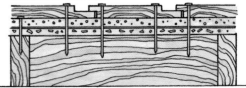

INSTALLING SIDING
continued

■ At gable ends determine the angle of the roof from its slope (see table, page 88) and cut the siding at this angle. Cut the board long and trim the bottom to fit.
■ Caulk corners before trimming.

HORIZONTAL WOOD SIDING: NAILING PATTERNS

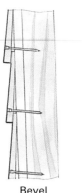
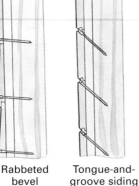
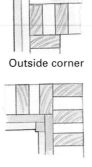

| Bevel siding | Rabbeted bevel siding | Tongue-and-groove siding | V-groove siding |

CORNER CONSTRUCTION

Outside corner

Inside corner

HORIZONTAL WOOD SIDING: CORNER TREATMENTS

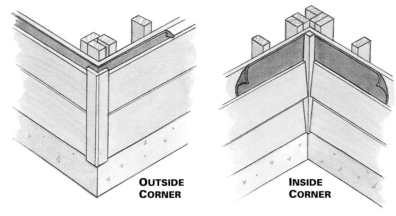

OUTSIDE CORNER

INSIDE CORNER

■ You can install horizontal siding directly over the studs, but sheathing minimizes waviness caused by out-of-plane studs.
■ Using a story pole (see opposite page), mark the studs or sheathing, and snap chalk lines at the marks.
■ Install flashing at door and window openings.
■ For beveled siding, install water table board or starter strip to tilt out the bottom board.
■ Align the bottom board on the first chalk line and nail it with 8d finish nails (see illustration at left). Predrill for nails at edges.
■ Align successive courses with the chalk lines.
■ At gables mark the edges of the boards with the angle for the slope (see table, page 88), and cut board in the middle to fit.
■ If installing vertical siding on the gable, flash the gap before siding the gable.

SHINGLES AND SHAKES

■ Mark the sheathing with a story pole (see opposite page) so shingles line up with the bottom of the windowsill and top of the window drip cap.
■ Flash the windows and doors with 4- to 6-inch shingle flashing or Z-flashing and 6-inch galvanized flashing.
■ Install water table board or starter strip.

SHIPLAP AND TONGUE-AND-GROOVE SIDING: BOTTOM TREATMENTS

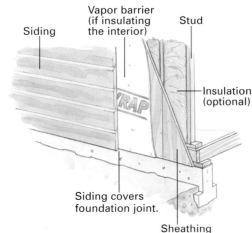

Siding

Vapor barrier (if insulating the interior)

Stud

Insulation (optional)

Siding covers foundation joint.

Sheathing

BEVEL SIDING: BOTTOM TREATMENTS

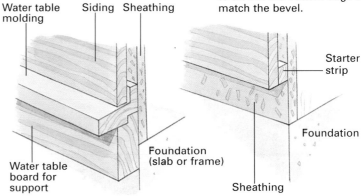

Water table molding

Siding

Sheathing

Water table board for support

Foundation (slab or frame)

Begin bevel siding with a water table molding or a starter strip to tilt out the bottom edge to match the bevel.

Starter strip

Foundation

Sheathing

SIDING RAKES AND EAVES

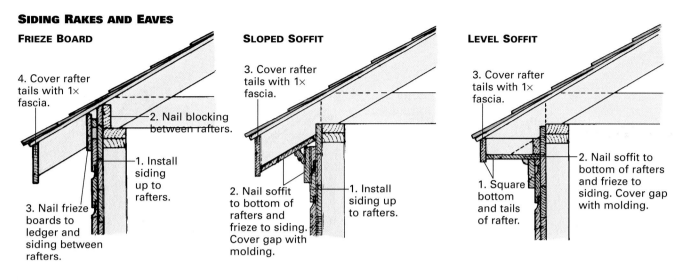

FRIEZE BOARD

4. Cover rafter tails with 1× fascia.

2. Nail blocking between rafters.

1. Install siding up to rafters.

3. Nail frieze boards to ledger and siding between rafters.

SLOPED SOFFIT

3. Cover rafter tails with 1× fascia.

2. Nail soffit to bottom of rafters and frieze to siding. Cover gap with molding.

1. Install siding up to rafters.

LEVEL SOFFIT

3. Cover rafter tails with 1× fascia.

1. Square bottom and tails of rafter.

2. Nail soffit to bottom of rafters and frieze to siding. Cover gap with molding.

■ Nail shingles at each end and stretch a mason's line between them. Nail the starter course along the line with galvanized ringshank nails 1 inch above the butt line and ¾ inch in from edges.

■ Nail the first course on the starter course.

■ Nail remaining courses aligned with the chalk lines.

■ Space kiln-dried shingles ⅛ inch apart and offset spaces 1½ inches from the course below. Don't line up a gap at the edge of a window or door.

■ Trim shingles from the butt end.

■ Finish inside and outside corners as shown at right. Caulk between shingles and corner boards.

■ Trim the final course to fit, and finish with 1×4 trim or molding to cover the gap at the soffit.

MAKING A STORY POLE

A story pole helps you line up horizontal siding boards.

Cut a straight 1×4 to fit from just below the bottom edge of the sheathing to the top of the wall. Stand the pole against the wall next to a window. Mark the board at the top and bottom of the sheathing and the top and bottom of the window. Divide the height of the sheathing by the maximum exposure of your siding. Round up fractions to determine the number of courses. Adjust the exposure to minimize cut siding above and below the windows, and mark the story pole at even increments. Use the pole to mark the sheathing at both ends of the wall; snap chalk lines between the marks.

INSTALLING WOOD SHINGLE SIDING

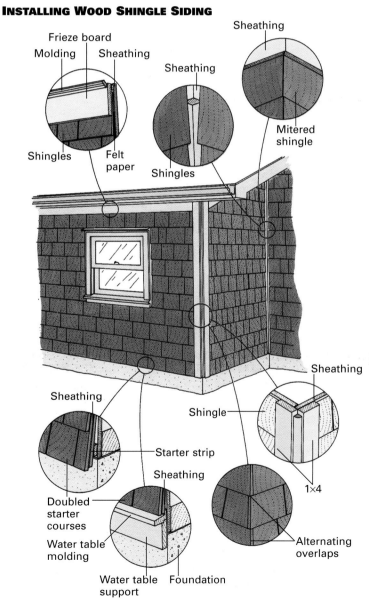

Frieze board

Molding

Sheathing

Shingles

Felt paper

Sheathing

Sheathing

Shingles

Sheathing

Mitered shingle

Sheathing

Sheathing

Starter strip

Sheathing

Doubled starter courses

Water table molding

Water table support

Foundation

Shingle

Sheathing

1×4

Alternating overlaps

INSTALLING A DOOR

The door to your shed or gazebo has a number of purposes. It encloses the structure, provides security, and adds to the structure's style. Its contribution to the design of your structure is second only to the style of the roof.

CHOOSING THE RIGHT DOOR

The first consideration in choosing a door is how you intend to use the structure. A simple potting shed or enclosed gazebo probably won't need extensive security, so any prehung single exterior door or even an all-weather storm door might be adequate. A garden shed where you'll park a riding mower and other motorized garden equipment, on the other hand, needs double doors wide enough to get the equipment through and substantial enough to resist intrusion. An outdoor workshop also needs secure double doors. For these installations you can build your own door.

PREHUNG OR DIY?

Prehung doors come complete with door, casing, and hardware already installed. The height, generally 80 to 82 inches, can be cut down. Most commercial exterior doors are 32 or 36 inches wide. Follow the manufacturer's instructions and the illustrations below to install a prehung door.

Do-it-yourself shed doors are built on a Z or X frame made of 2× stock, with 1× or 2× facing, as shown on the opposite page. You can also make your own door from ¾-inch plywood reinforced with battens. Determine the finished size of a door before you build the framing so you can make the rough opening the right size.

HANGING A DOOR

1. Flash door with 15-lb. felt paper, overlapping the sheets.

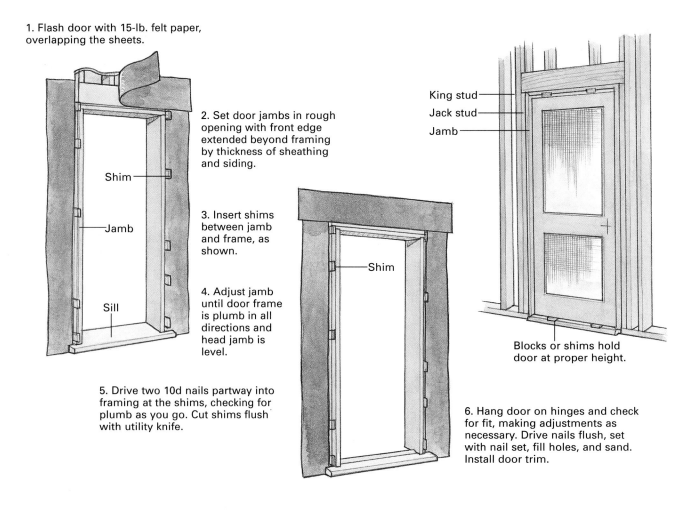

Shim

Jamb

Sill

2. Set door jambs in rough opening with front edge extended beyond framing by thickness of sheathing and siding.

3. Insert shims between jamb and frame, as shown.

Shim

4. Adjust jamb until door frame is plumb in all directions and head jamb is level.

5. Drive two 10d nails partway into framing at the shims, checking for plumb as you go. Cut shims flush with utility knife.

King stud
Jack stud
Jamb

Blocks or shims hold door at proper height.

6. Hang door on hinges and check for fit, making adjustments as necessary. Drive nails flush, set with nail set, fill holes, and sand. Install door trim.

DESIGNING YOUR OWN DOORS

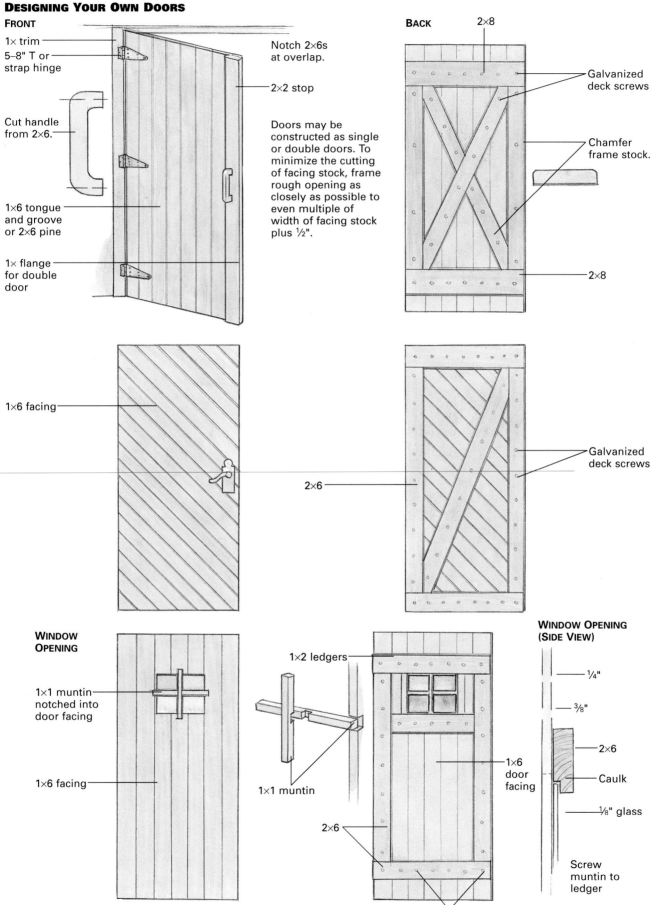

FRONT

1× trim

5–8" T or strap hinge

Cut handle from 2×6.

1×6 tongue and groove or 2×6 pine

1× flange for double door

Notch 2×6s at overlap.

2×2 stop

Doors may be constructed as single or double doors. To minimize the cutting of facing stock, frame rough opening as closely as possible to even multiple of width of facing stock plus ½".

BACK

2×8

Galvanized deck screws

Chamfer frame stock.

2×8

1×6 facing

2×6

Galvanized deck screws

WINDOW OPENING

1×1 muntin notched into door facing

1×6 facing

1×2 ledgers

1×1 muntin

1×6 door facing

2×6

Galvanized deck screws

WINDOW OPENING (SIDE VIEW)

¼"

⅜"

2×6

Caulk

⅛" glass

Screw muntin to ledger

INSTALLING WINDOWS

FLASHING A WINDOW

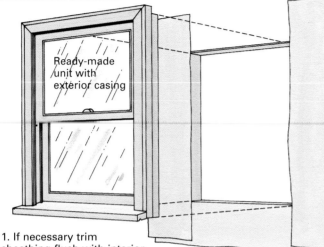

Ready-made unit with exterior casing

1. If necessary trim sheathing flush with interior of the opening. For windows with brick mold, trim back sheathing to exterior dimensions of brick mold.

2. Staple 15-lb. felt paper to bottom, sides, and top of window, overlapping the pieces.

3. Cut Z-flashing to width of window plus 1 inch and fasten it to sheathing or slide it under siding.

INSTALLING A STANDARD WINDOW

1. Set window in rough opening flush with the thickness of siding.

2. Center window in opening.

3. Insert shims every 12" between window and framing.

4. Level the sill and plumb the sides. Drive two 10d finishing nails partway into framing at shims.

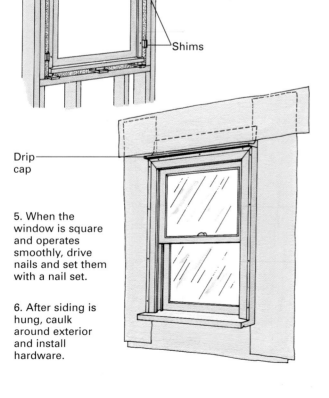

INTERIOR VIEW

Shims

Drip cap

5. When the window is square and operates smoothly, drive nails and set them with a nail set.

6. After siding is hung, caulk around exterior and install hardware.

Hunting for a garden tool in the dark can be frustrating. In most cases windows will provide ample light and a cheery environment in your shed, but you can electrify the structure if you like.

WINDOW STYLES

You can install in a shed almost any window made for a house. Start by looking at your local home center. Retailers usually have a variety of styles—double-hung (both sashes slide up and down to open), casement (open on one side), hoppers (hinge at the bottom), and even bay windows.

Most commercial windows come complete with casings, sill, and hardware. If it's compatible with your design and you want to avoid delivery delays, order a standard size and design your rough opening to the manufacturer's specifications.

Don't overlook local salvage yards as an excellent source for windows that can add unique accents to your shed. If you find a metal or flanged window you like, inspect it carefully. It's hard to remove these windows without damaging them, and most damage is impossible to repair. Wood windows are a better bet. You can even take apart double-hung units and use each sash separately.

INSTALLATION

Most windows are installed by nailing through the casing or a nailing flange. Directions for each style are illustrated on this page.

INSTALLING A WINDOW WITH A NAILING FLANGE

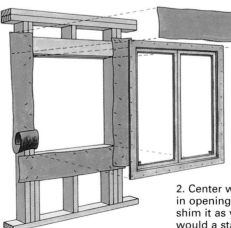

4. Staple top strip of felt paper over nailing flange.

3. Nail or screw through holes in nailing flange.

2. Center window in opening and shim it as you would a standard window.

1. Staple bottom and sides of opening with 15-lb. felt paper.

ALTERNATE WINDOW DESIGNS

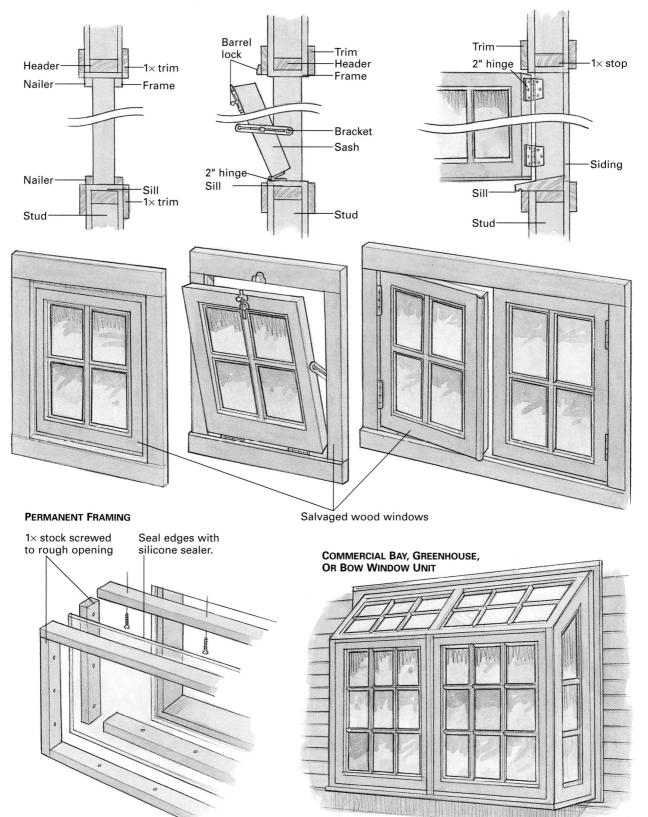

Header — 1× trim
Nailer — Frame

Nailer — Sill
Stud — 1× trim

Barrel lock — Trim
Header
Frame
Bracket
Sash
2" hinge —
Sill — Stud

Trim — 1× stop
2" hinge
Siding
Sill —
Stud —

Salvaged wood windows

PERMANENT FRAMING

1× stock screwed to rough opening — Seal edges with silicone sealer.

COMMERCIAL BAY, GREENHOUSE, OR BOW WINDOW UNIT

INSTALLING WINDOWS
continued

MEASURING FOR WINDOW TRIM

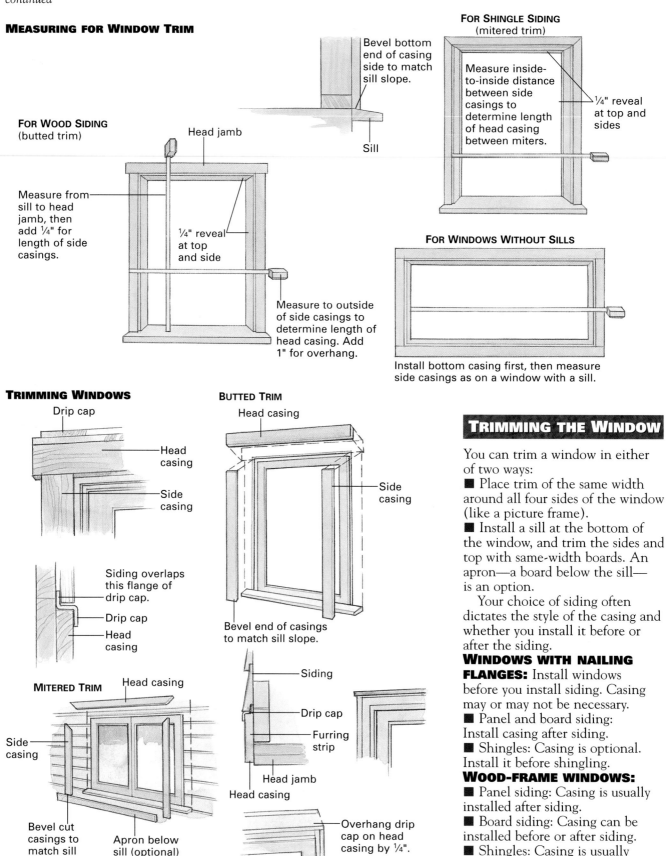

Bevel bottom end of casing side to match sill slope.

Sill

FOR WOOD SIDING (butted trim)

Head jamb

Measure from sill to head jamb, then add ¼" for length of side casings.

¼" reveal at top and side

Measure to outside of side casings to determine length of head casing. Add 1" for overhang.

FOR SHINGLE SIDING (mitered trim)

Measure inside-to-inside distance between side casings to determine length of head casing between miters.

¼" reveal at top and sides

FOR WINDOWS WITHOUT SILLS

Install bottom casing first, then measure side casings as on a window with a sill.

TRIMMING WINDOWS

Drip cap

Head casing

Side casing

Siding overlaps this flange of drip cap.

Drip cap

Head casing

MITERED TRIM

Head casing

Side casing

Bevel cut casings to match sill slope.

Apron below sill (optional)

BUTTED TRIM

Head casing

Side casing

Bevel end of casings to match sill slope.

Siding

Drip cap

Furring strip

Head jamb

Head casing

Overhang drip cap on head casing by ¼".

TRIMMING THE WINDOW

You can trim a window in either of two ways:
- Place trim of the same width around all four sides of the window (like a picture frame).
- Install a sill at the bottom of the window, and trim the sides and top with same-width boards. An apron—a board below the sill—is an option.

Your choice of siding often dictates the style of the casing and whether you install it before or after the siding.

WINDOWS WITH NAILING FLANGES: Install windows before you install siding. Casing may or may not be necessary.
- Panel and board siding: Install casing after siding.
- Shingles: Casing is optional. Install it before shingling.

WOOD-FRAME WINDOWS:
- Panel siding: Casing is usually installed after siding.
- Board siding: Casing can be installed before or after siding.
- Shingles: Casing is usually installed before siding.

PAINTS AND STAINS

The right finish protects your structure and helps it fit into your landscape. Focus first on color, tone, and surface sheen (flat or glossy) when deciding on a finish. Then look for durability and ease of application. Consider the wood too. A clear finish allows redwood and cedar to show off their natural colors, while treated lumber usually requires staining or painting.

SEALERS: Clear or lightly pigmented sealers resist water damage. They protect the wood but don't change its color much. Additives ward off mildew, insects, and fungi, and ultraviolet (UV) blockers reduce damage caused by the sun. Pigmented sealers do the same thing but also change the color of the wood slightly. All-purpose sealers contain water repellents, preservatives, and UV blockers. You can apply sealers over or under stains and under primer and paint.

PAINTS: Paints conceal some defects and tend to last longer and look better than stains on smooth surfaces. Exterior alkyds, oil-base products, are more costly, more difficult to clean up, and slower drying. Water-base latex paints cost less, clean up easily, and dry quickly. Each comes in a range of colors and sheens (gloss, semigloss, and flat or matte). New, unpainted surfaces need to be primed first. Oil-base primers provide better protection on raw wood than water-base primers. Add stain-blockers to stop bleed-through from redwood and cedar. A good-quality acrylic-latex top coat applied over an alkyd primer makes a durable finish.

STAINS: Stains protect the wood's surface but also transform its appearance. They are somewhat less expensive than paints, take less time to apply, and go on easily over rough and smooth surfaces. Semitransparent stains allow more wood grain to show through but wear away more quickly; they are particularly suitable for highlighting wood grains. Heavy-body stains contain more pigments and hide the grain. All stains tend to retain the wood's natural look. Apply oil-base stains on redwood and red cedar.

BLEACHING, WEATHERING STAINS: Bleaching treatments don't protect the wood but they lighten its natural tones. They offer an intermediate solution to the problem of toning down the look of a brand-new structure. Bleaching treatments strip color from the wood fibers, providing the effect of two seasons of natural weathering in one application. Note that some products are harmful to plants and grasses. Also, sealers interfere with the bleach, so bleach wood before sealing or finishing it.

A carefully chosen color scheme helps the structure blend into the rest of your landscape to minimize its presence.

The whimsical painting on this shed makes it an attention-getter in the garden. Here, the shed is an important accent in the garden design.

Stains accentuate the tones of the wood and give you a wide range of colors with which to complement nature's work. Protect stained surfaces with sealers or other finishes.

GLOSSARY

ACTUAL DIMENSIONS: The exact measurements of a piece of lumber after it has been surfaced and dried.

BALUSTER: A vertical member of a rail assembly installed between upper and lower rails.

BATTEN: A strip of wood used to hide a seam or to reinforce another board.

BEAM: A framing member used to support joists.

BIRD'S MOUTH: A notch in a rafter that allows it to rest squarely on the top or cap plate.

CAP PLATE: A horizontal framing member fastened to the top of a top plate, used to tie adjacent walls together.

CASING: The framing of a window or door.

CHALK LINE: Chalked cord snapped against a surface to mark a line, or the line made this way.

CLAPBOARD: Horizontal wood siding whose bottom edge is thicker than the top edge.

COMMON RAFTER: A rafter that runs from ridge to bird's mouth.

COMPOSITE SHINGLES: Roofing material made of asphalt and fiberglass.

CURING: Chemical action that hardens concrete.

DECK HEIGHT: The distance from the ground to the top of the decking.

DECKING: Floor covering, generally 1× or 2× lumber nailed to joists.

DRIP CAP: An aluminum or steel strip installed above a window or door to divert rain.

EAVE: The edge of a roof along its longest dimension.

FACE-NAIL: To fasten boards together by driving nails through the face of one into the end, edge, or face of another.

FASCIA: A horizontal board fastened to the ends of rafters.

FRAMING SQUARE: An L-shape tool used to mark right angles, check for square, and lay out rafters.

FRIEZE: A horizontal band fastened near the roofline.

FROST HEAVE: Rapid expansion of the ground surface caused by alternate freezing and thawing of water in the soil.

FROST LINE: The maximum depth at which soil freezes in winter; varies by location.

GABLE ROOF: A roof with two surfaces that form triangles at the ends.

GALVANIZED: A term describing the zinc coating on metals used to prevent rust.

GRADE: Ground level.

HARDWOOD: Wood cut from deciduous trees (those that lose their leaves).

HEADER: A heavy beam, often of doubled 2× stock, placed across window and door openings to support weight above.

HIP RAFTER: A rafter running diagonally from the ridge to the corners of a building.

HURRICANE TIES: Framing connectors used to secure rafters to top plates.

JACK RAFTERS: Short rafters that run between a hip rafter and cap plate or from the ridge to the main roof in a dormer.

JOIST: A framing member that supports flooring.

KERF: The wood removed by a saw blade.

KICKBACK: The action of a circular saw when it binds or is otherwise obstructed in the cut.

LOOKOUTS: Short beams that support the overhang of a roof on the gable ends.

MITER JOINT: A joint whose sides are cut at equal angles.

NAIL SET: A steel tool used to drive nails below the surface of a board.

NOMINAL DIMENSIONS: The dimensions of a piece of lumber representing the proportion of one side to the other; the measurement before surfacing and drying.

PLUMB: Perfectly vertical.

POST ANCHORS: Connectors that secure a post to a concrete slab, pier, or deck.

PRE-MIXED CONCRETE: Dry concrete materials mixed in correct proportion and sold in bags.

PRESSURE-TREATED LUMBER: Lumber infused with chemicals to make it resistant to moisture or insect damage.

PRIMARY COLORS: Pure red, blue, and yellow hues that cannot be derived from other colors.

PRIMER: An undercoat of paint used to provide a bonding surface for finish coats.

RAFTER TAIL: The length of rafter that overhangs the wall.

RAFTER TIES: Boards fastened to the ends of rafters above the cap plate and used to keep the weight of a roof from spreading the walls. Also called collar ties.

RAIL: A horizontal member of a wall, window, or door.

RAKE: The edge of a roof along its shorter dimension.

READY-MIX CONCRETE: Mixed concrete delivered by truck.

RIDGE: The top horizontal member of the roof. Also the line formed by this board.

RIM JOIST: Outermost joist of a structure.

RISE: The vertical distance from the top of a wall to the roof peak.

RUN: The horizontal distance over which a framing member rises.

SCREED: To strike concrete level in the forms by sliding a straightedge across the form tops.

SHIPLAP: Board siding rabbeted along one edge to make a flush joint.

SKEW: To drive fasteners at an opposing angle. Used to strengthen joints.

SLOPE: The amount a roof rises, expressed as inches of rise per inches of run.

SOFFIT: The underside of rafters at the eave.

SOFTWOOD: Wood that comes from evergreen trees (those that do not lose their leaves).

SPAN: The horizontal distance covered by a framing member.

SQUARE: To form a right angle. Also refers to a measure of area, commonly 100 square feet.

TOENAIL: To fasten two boards together by driving fasteners at an angle through the end of one board into the face of another.

TOP PLATE: The horizontal framing member that forms the top of a wall.

USDA PLANT HARDINESS ZONE MAP

This map of climate zones helps you select plants for your garden that will survive a typical winter in your region. The United States Department of Agriculture (USDA) developed the map, basing the zones on the lowest recorded temperatures across North America. Zone 1 is the coldest area and Zone 11 is the warmest.

Plants are classified by the coldest temperature and zone they can endure. For example, plants hardy to Zone 6 survive where winter temperatures drop to –10° F. Those hardy to Zone 8 die long before it gets that cold. These plants may grow in colder regions but must be replaced each year. Plants rated for a range of hardiness zones usually survive winter in the coldest region, as well as tolerate the summer heat of the warmest one.

To find your hardiness zone, note the approximate location of your community on the map, then match its color band to the key.

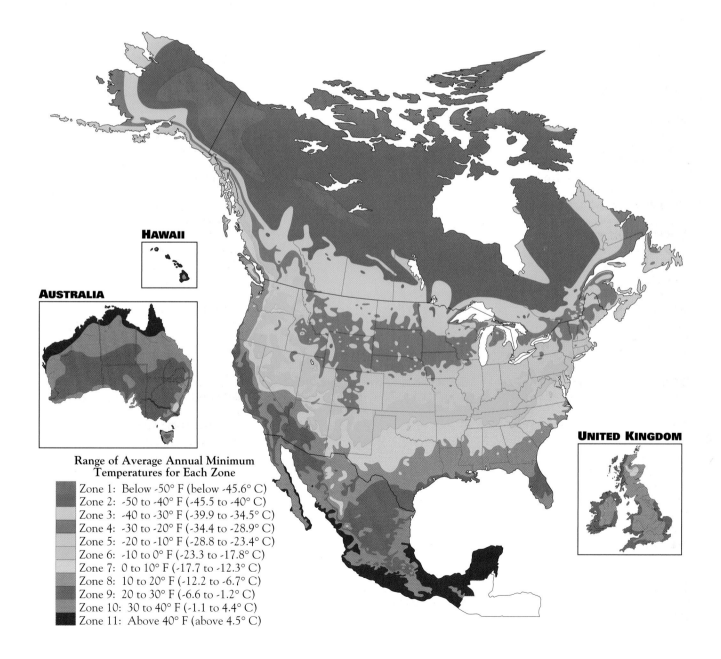

HAWAII

AUSTRALIA

UNITED KINGDOM

Range of Average Annual Minimum Temperatures for Each Zone

Zone 1: Below -50° F (below -45.6° C)
Zone 2: -50 to -40° F (-45.5 to -40° C)
Zone 3: -40 to -30° F (-39.9 to -34.5° C)
Zone 4: -30 to -20° F (-34.4 to -28.9° C)
Zone 5: -20 to -10° F (-28.8 to -23.4° C)
Zone 6: -10 to 0° F (-23.3 to -17.8° C)
Zone 7: 0 to 10° F (-17.7 to -12.3° C)
Zone 8: 10 to 20° F (-12.2 to -6.7° C)
Zone 9: 20 to 30° F (-6.6 to -1.2° C)
Zone 10: 30 to 40° F (-1.1 to 4.4° C)
Zone 11: Above 40° F (above 4.5° C)

INDEX

METRIC CONVERSIONS

U.S. Units to Metric Equivalents			Metric Units to U.S. Equivalents		
To Convert From	Multiply By	To Get	To Convert From	Multiply By	To Get
Inches	25.4	Millimeters	Millimeters	0.0394	Inches
Inches	2.54	Centimeters	Centimeters	0.3937	Inches
Feet	30.48	Centimeters	Centimeters	0.0328	Feet
Feet	0.3048	Meters	Meters	3.2808	Feet
Yards	0.9144	Meters	Meters	1.0936	Yards
Square inches	6.4516	Square centimeters	Square centimeters	0.1550	Square inches
Square feet	0.0929	Square meters	Square meters	10.764	Square feet
Square yards	0.8361	Square meters	Square meters	1.1960	Square yards
Acres	0.4047	Hectares	Hectares	2.4711	Acres
Cubic inches	16.387	Cubic centimeters	Cubic centimeters	0.0610	Cubic inches
Cubic feet	0.0283	Cubic meters	Cubic meters	35.315	Cubic feet
Cubic feet	28.316	Liters	Liters	0.0353	Cubic feet
Cubic yards	0.7646	Cubic meters	Cubic meters	1.308	Cubic yards
Cubic yards	764.55	Liters	Liters	0.0013	Cubic yards

To convert from degrees Fahrenheit (F) to degrees Celsius (C), first subtract 32, then multiply by $\frac{5}{9}$.

To convert from degrees Celsius to degrees Fahrenheit, multiply by $\frac{9}{5}$, then add 32.